AF469126

WHOOPS!

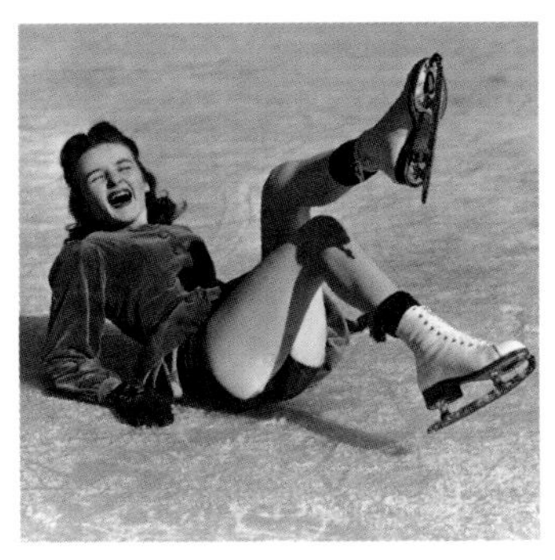

WHOOPS!

a photographic celebration

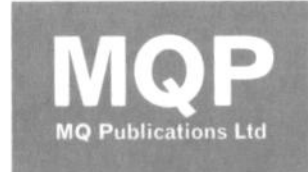

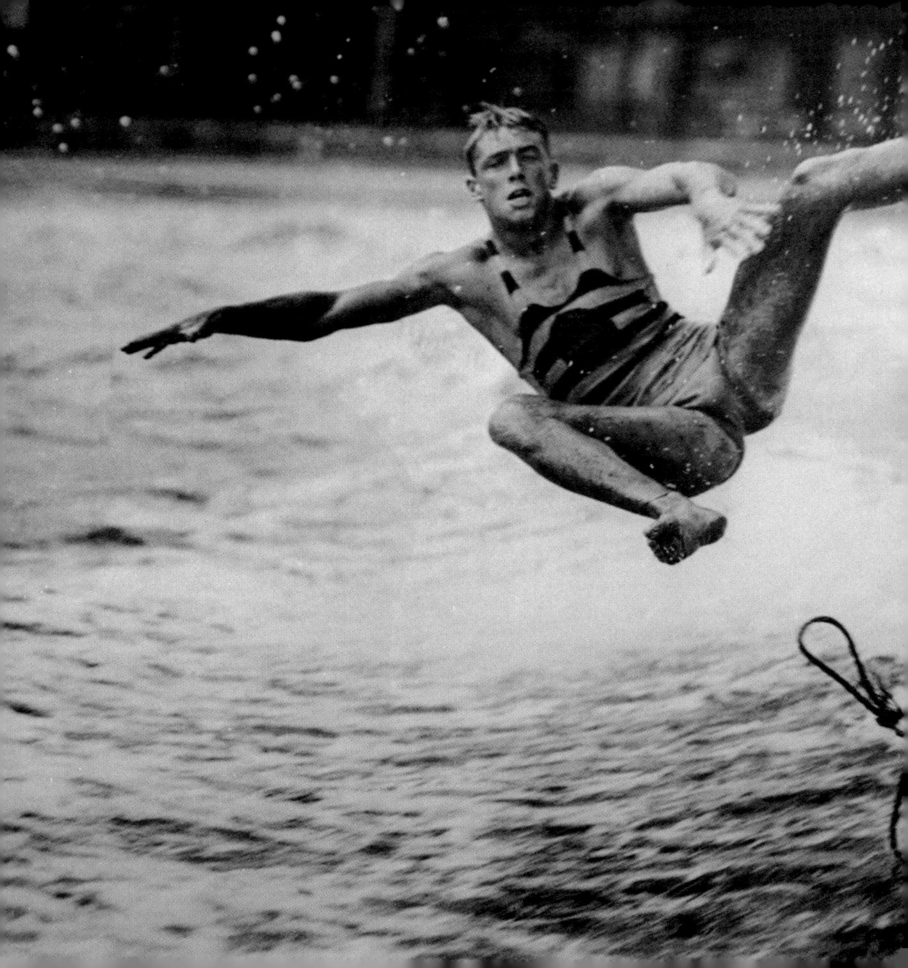

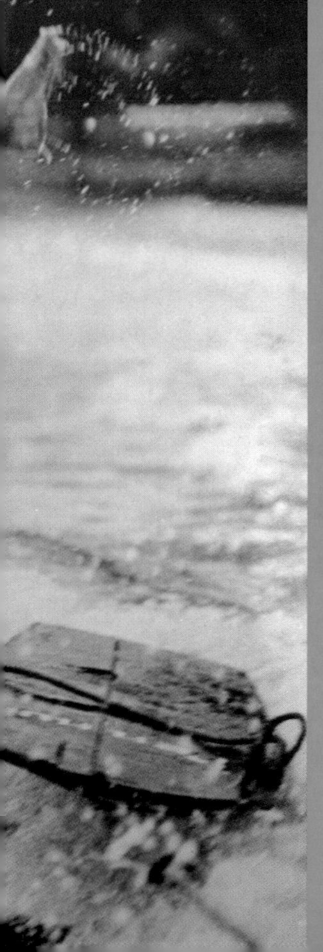

The first requisite for success
is the ability to apply your
physical and mental energies
to one problem incessantly
without growing weary.

Thomas Edison

A person without a sense of humor

is like a wagon without springs,

jolted by every pebble in the road.

Henry Ward Beecher

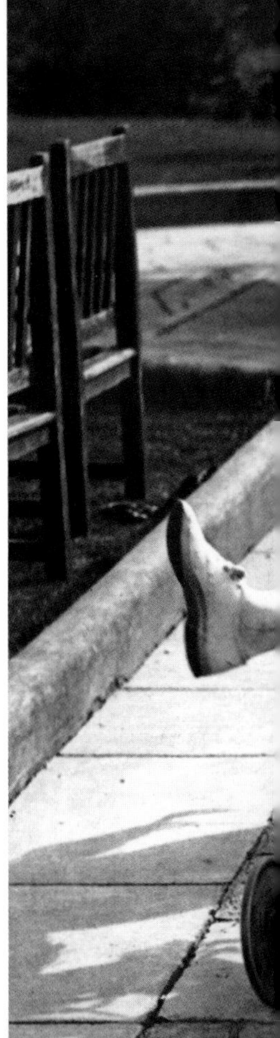

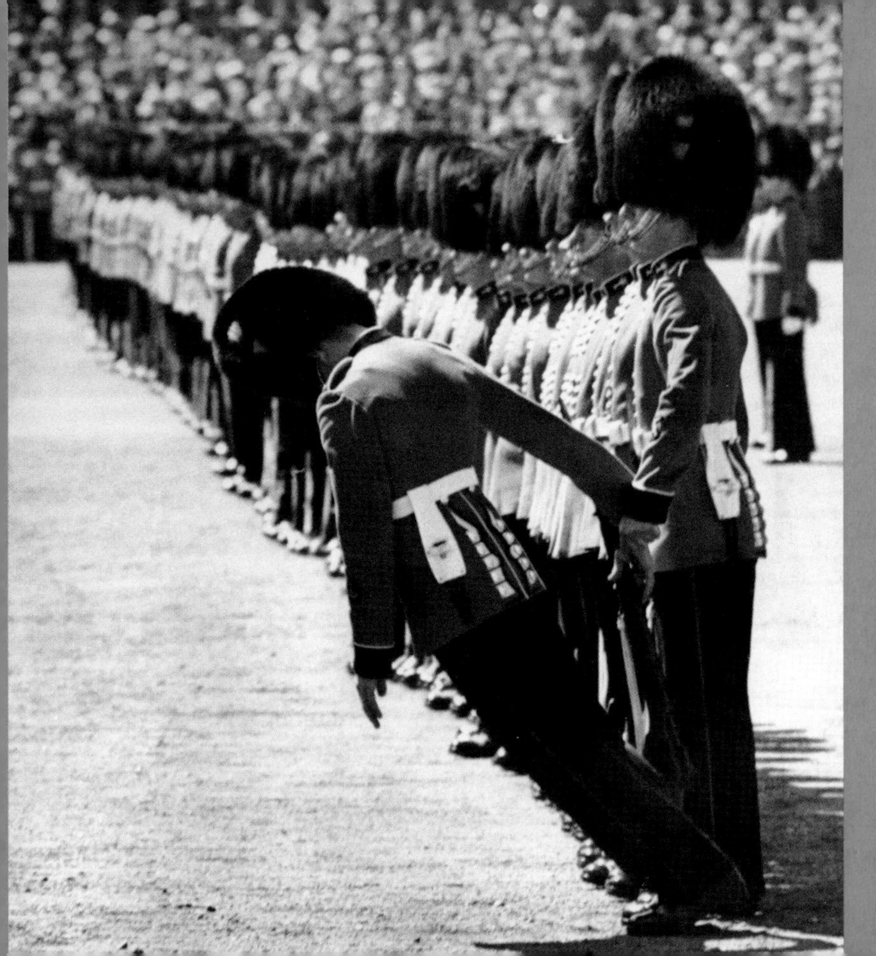

The important thing is not to stop questioning.

Curiosity has its own reason for existing.

Albert Einstein

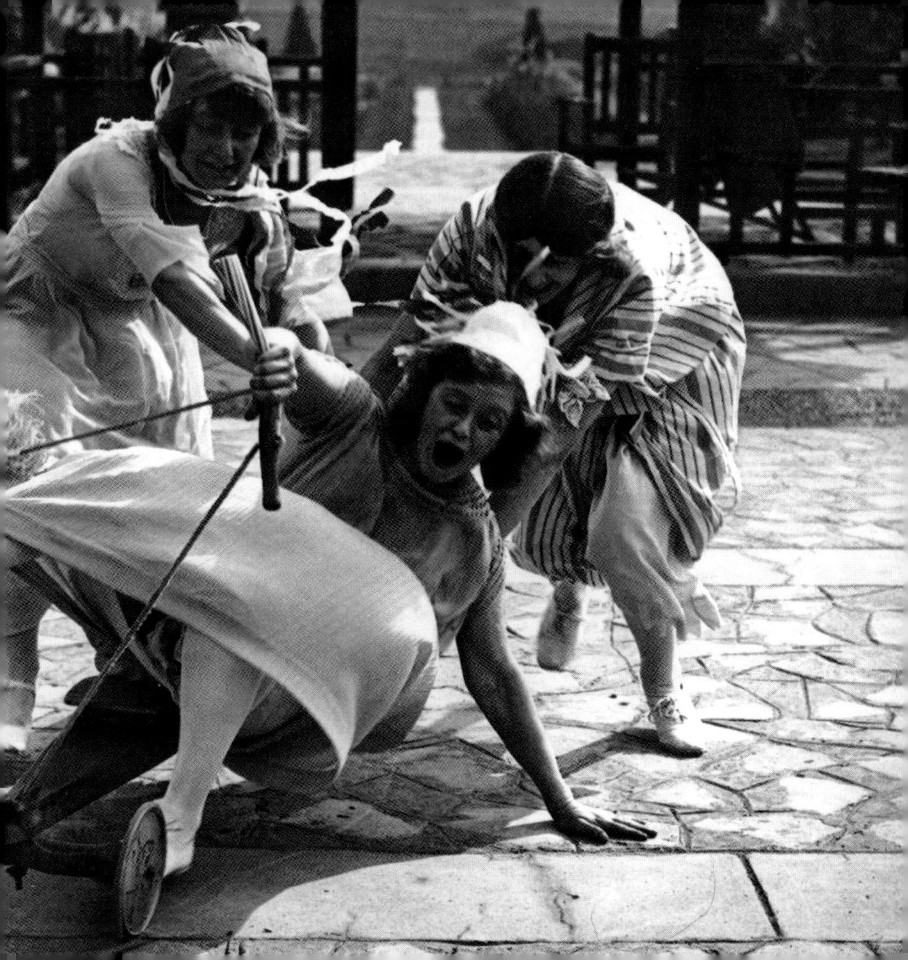

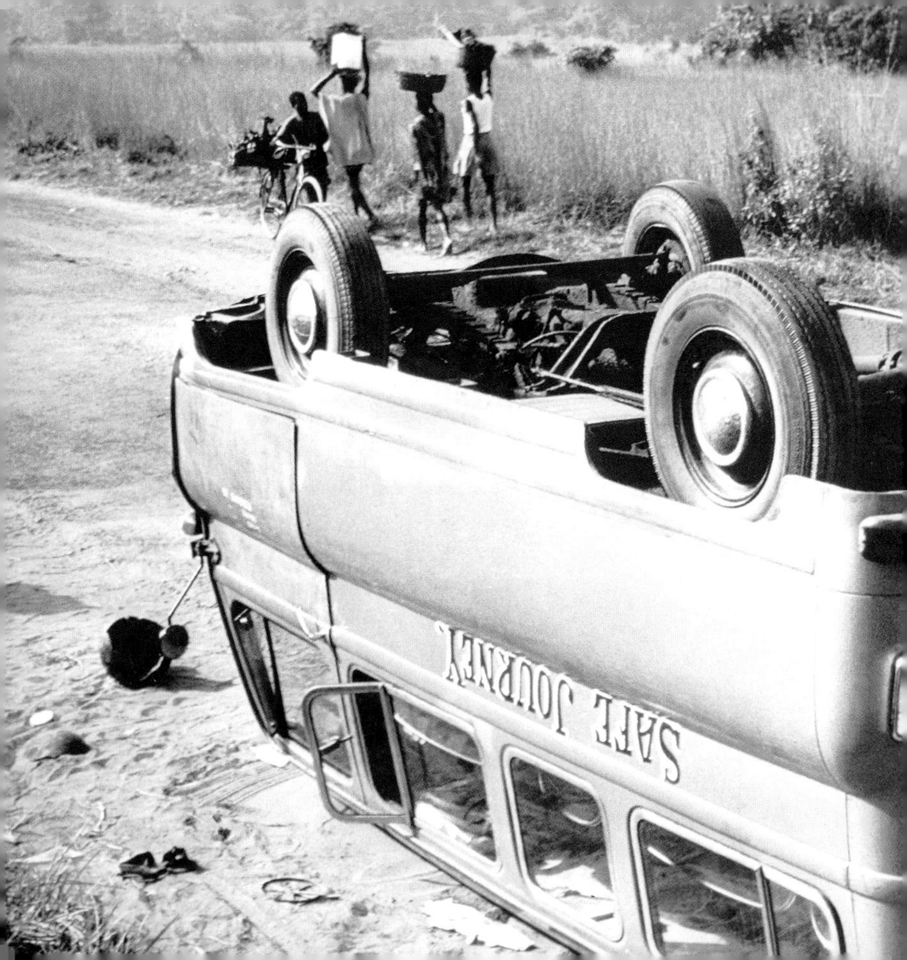
SAFE JOURNEY

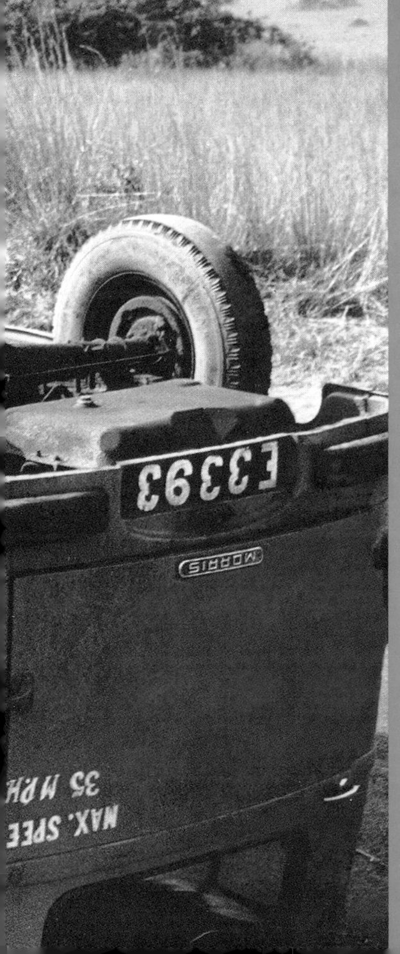

The difference between

stupidity and genius is

that genius has its limits.

Albert Einstein

I have seen that in any great undertaking it is not enough for a man to depend simply upon himself.

Lone Man (Isna-la-wica)
Teton Sioux

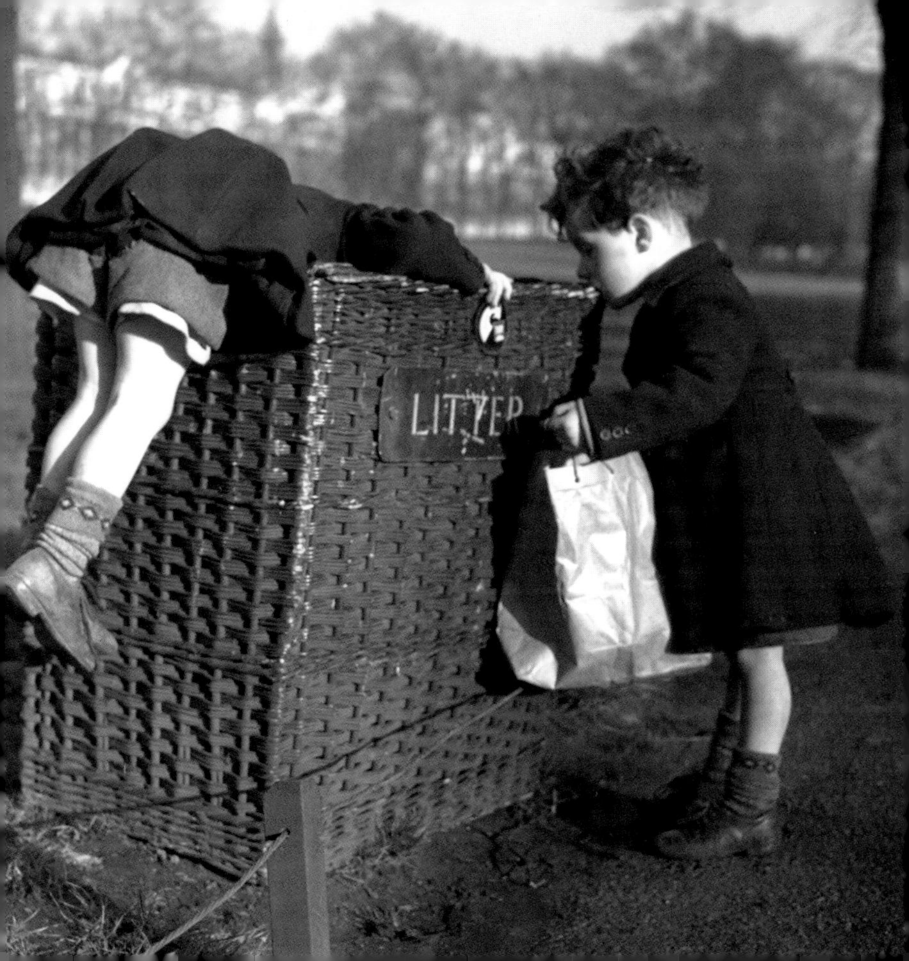
LITTER

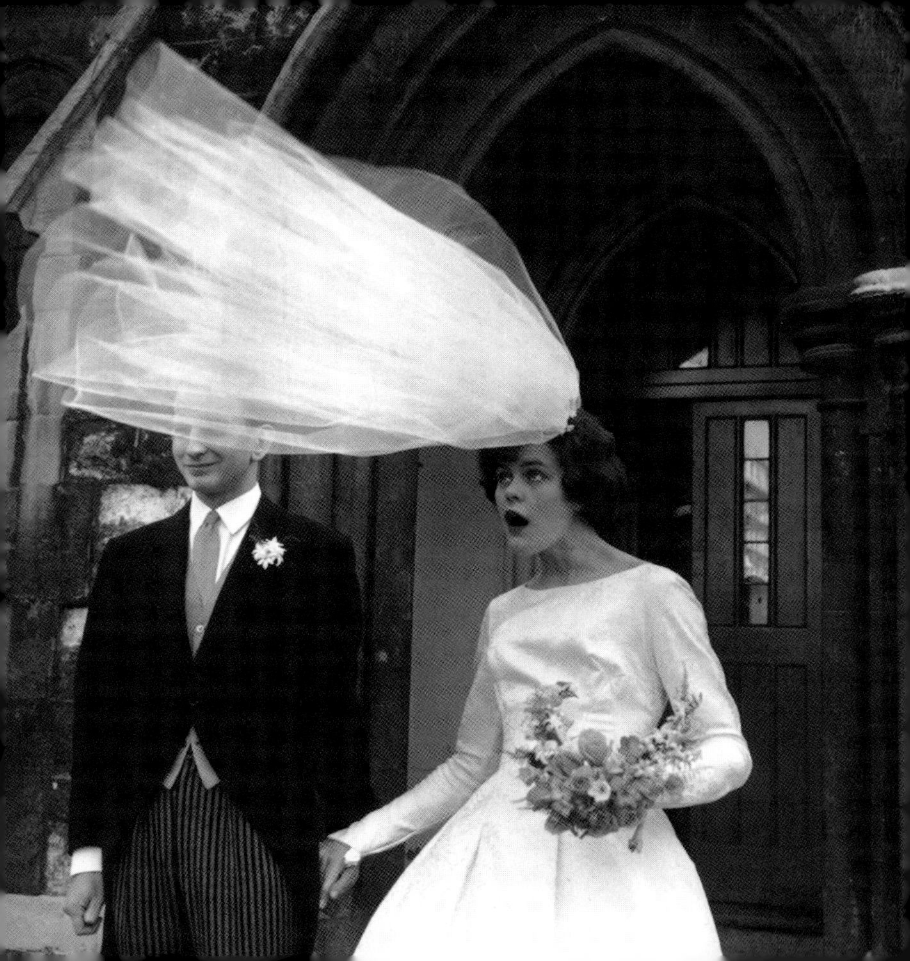

God, grant me serenity to accept the things I cannot change, courage to change the things I can, and the wisdom to know the difference.

Reinhold Niebuhr

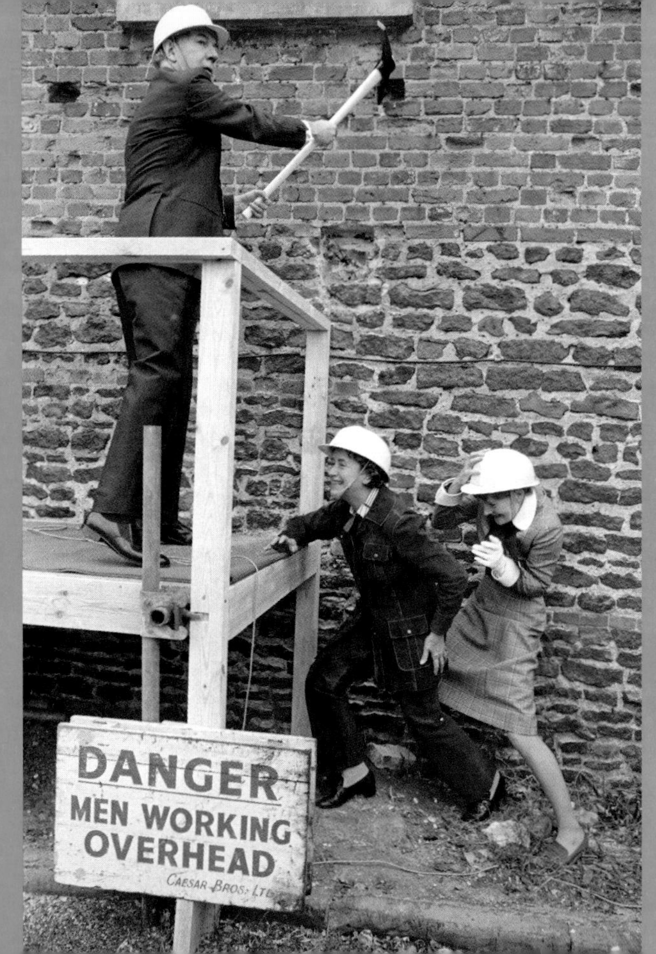
DANGER
MEN WORKING
OVERHEAD
CAESAR BROS. LTD

A successful person is one who can lay a firm foundation with the bricks that others throw at him or her.

David Brinkley

Everyone according to their talent and every talent according to its work.

French Proverb

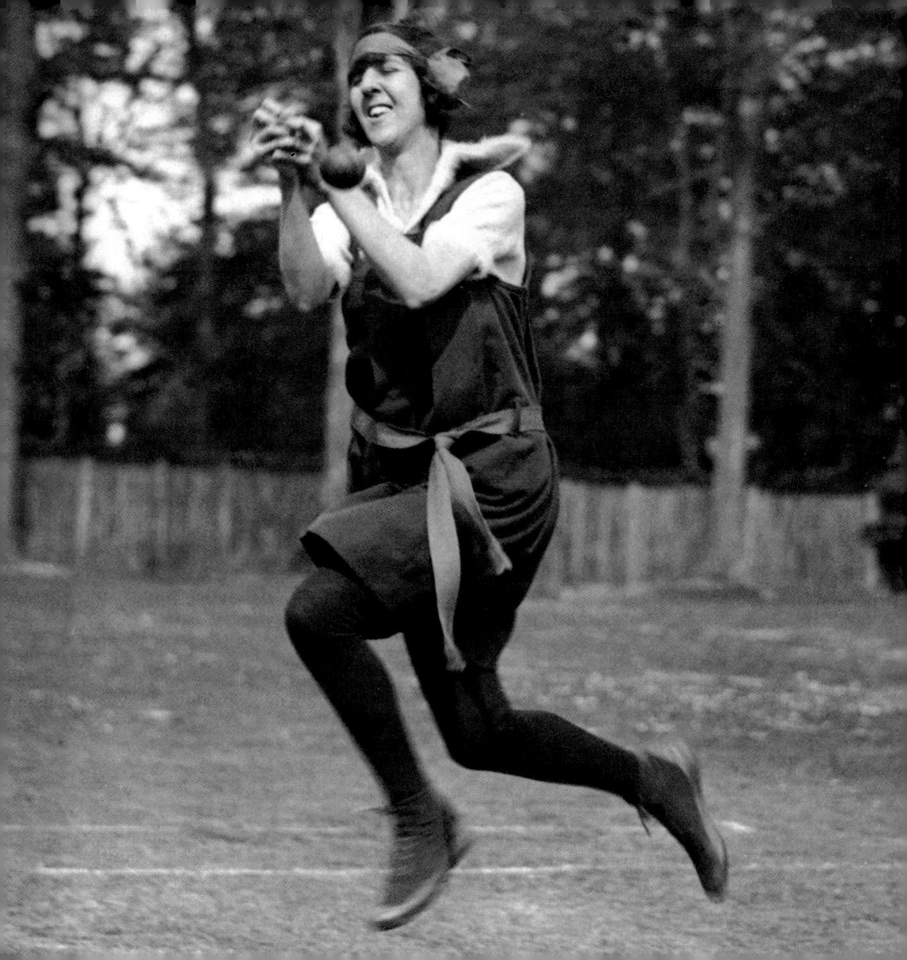

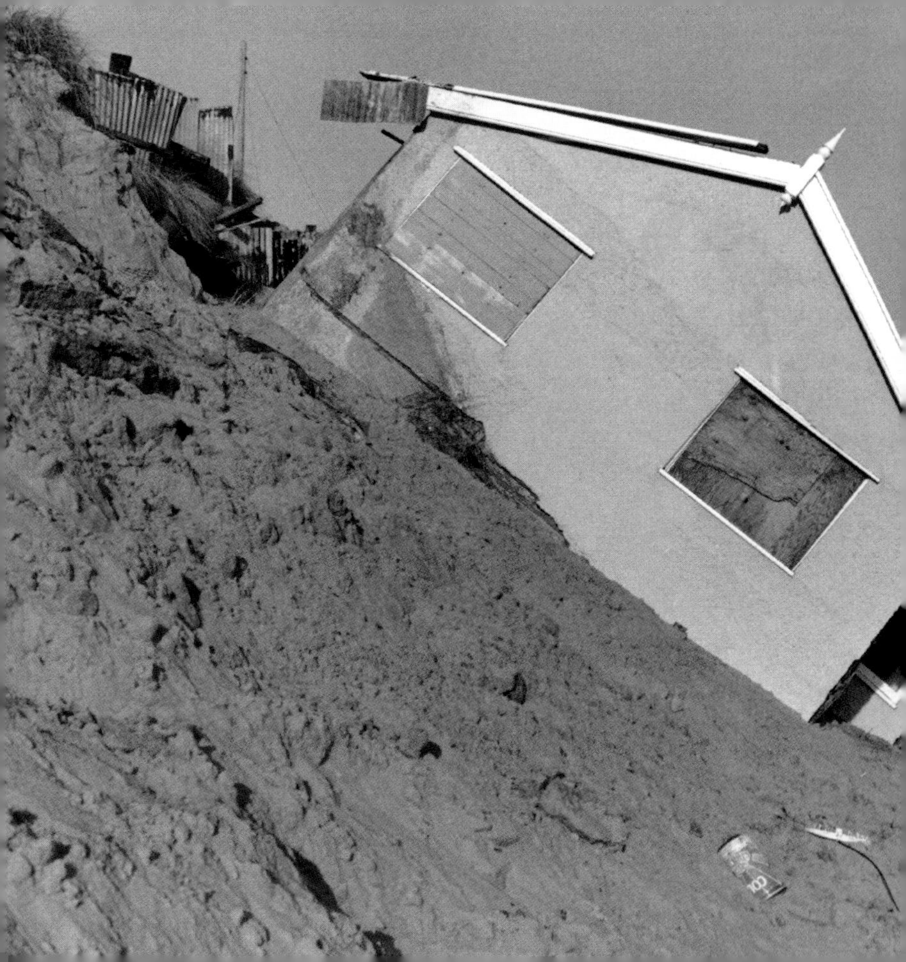

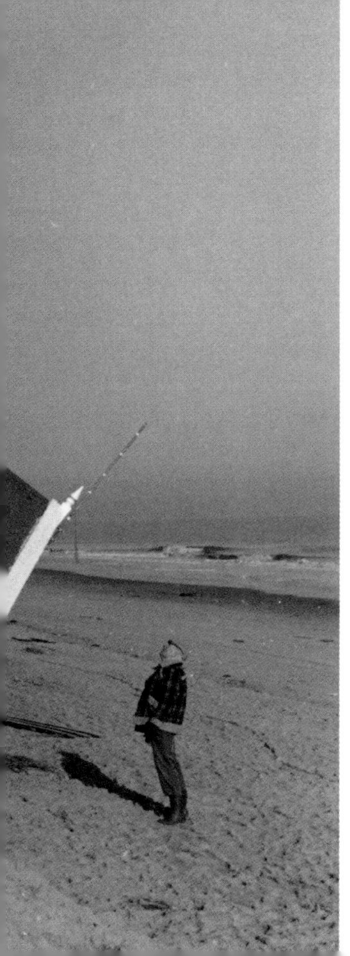

The intelligent man finds almost everything ridiculous, the sensible man hardly anything.

Johann Wolfgang von Goethe

If I am walking with two other men, each of them will serve as my teacher. I will pick out the good points of the one and imitate them, and the bad points of the other and correct them in myself.

Confucius

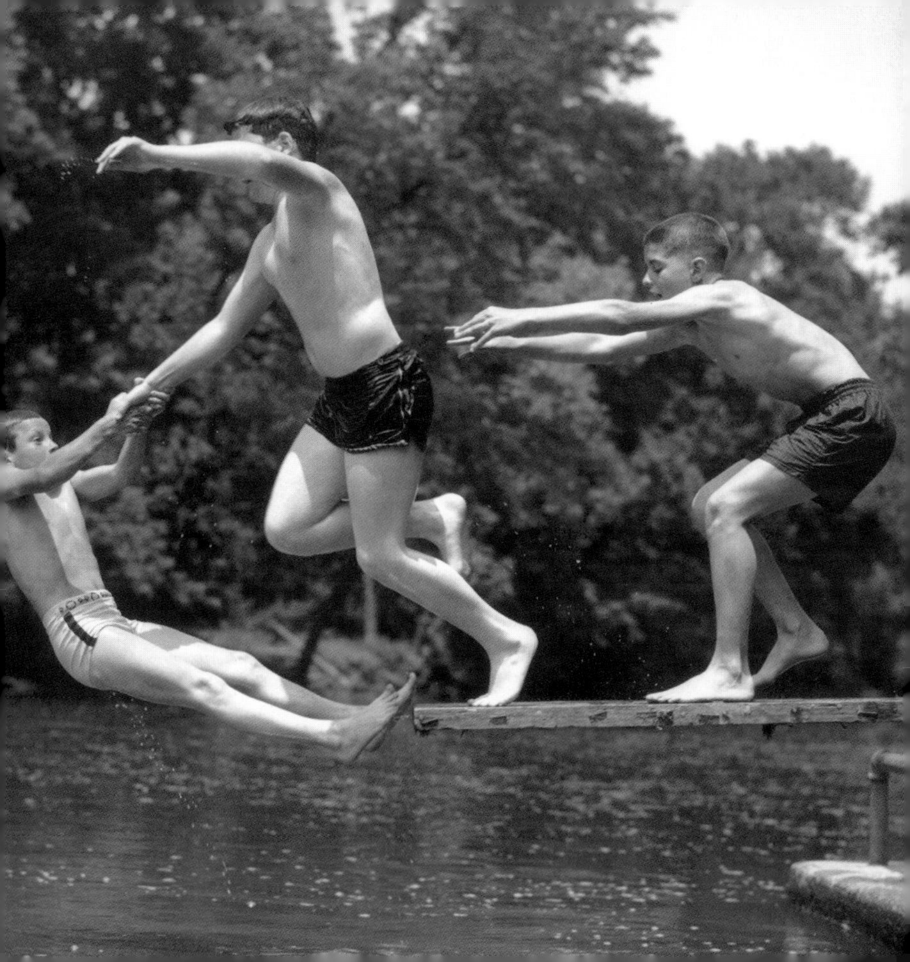

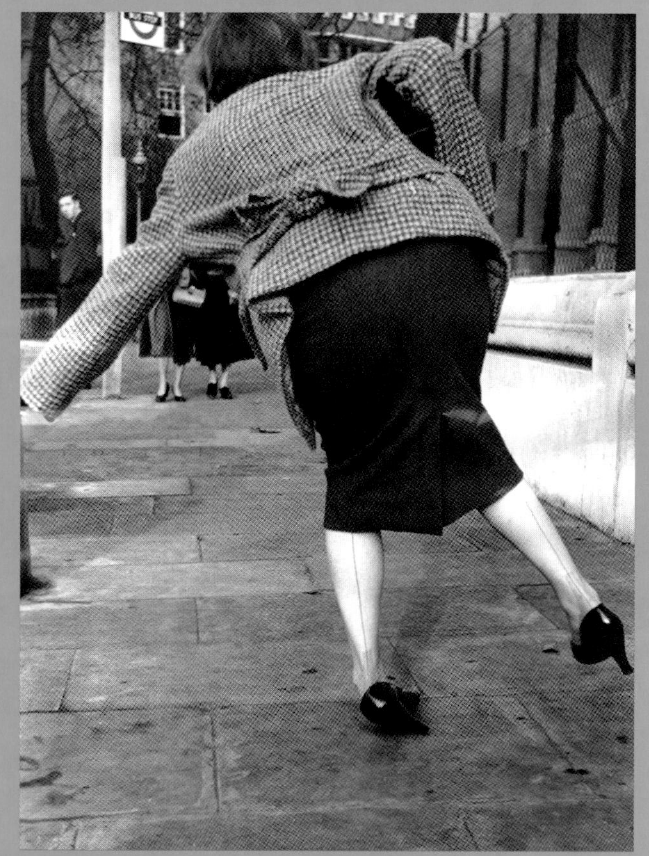

If you get up one more time than you fall you will make it through.

Chinese Proverb

Wisdom begins in wonder.

Socrates

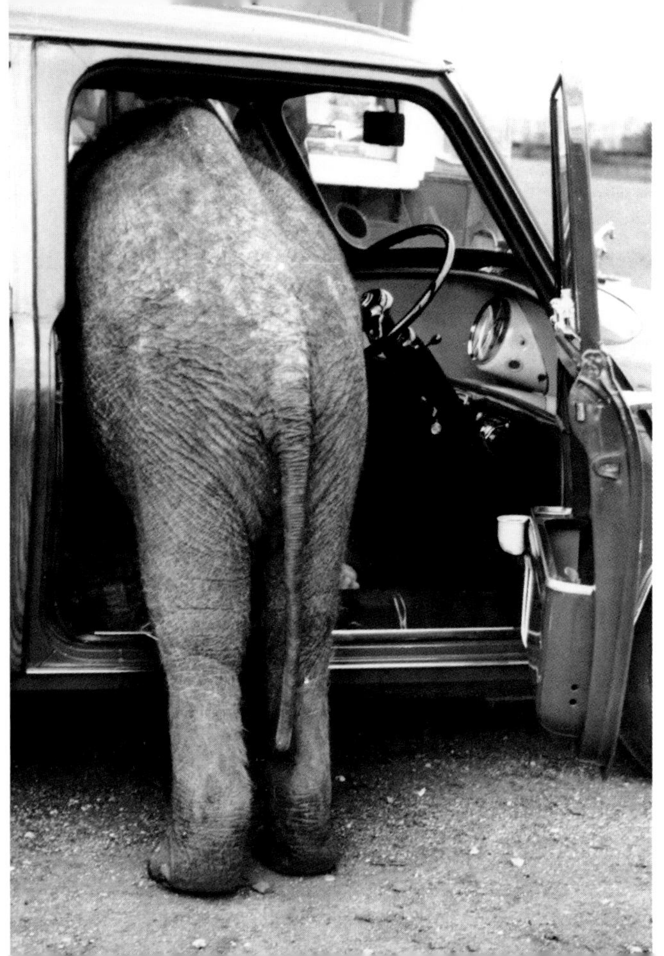

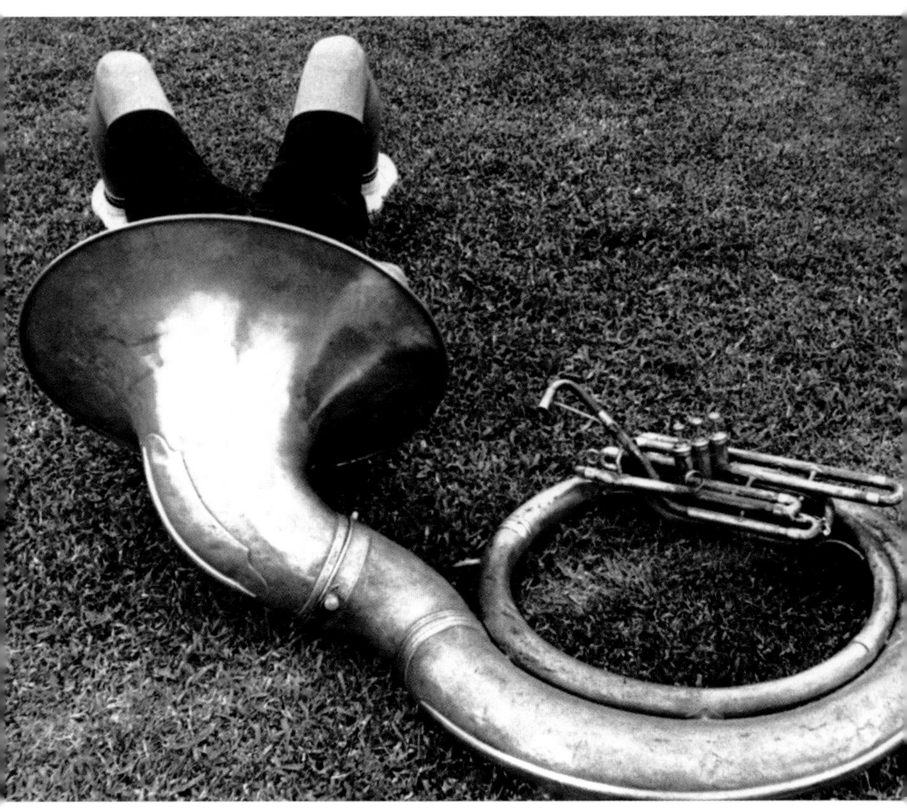

I'm always thinking about creating. My future starts when I wake up every morning. Every day I find something creative to do with my life.

Miles Davis

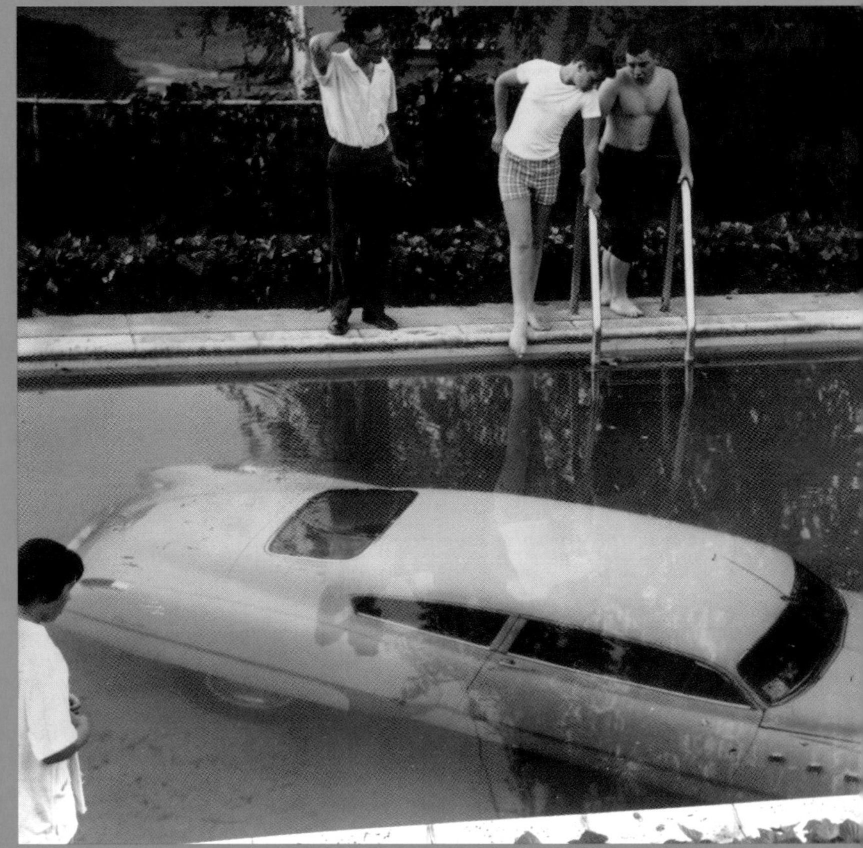

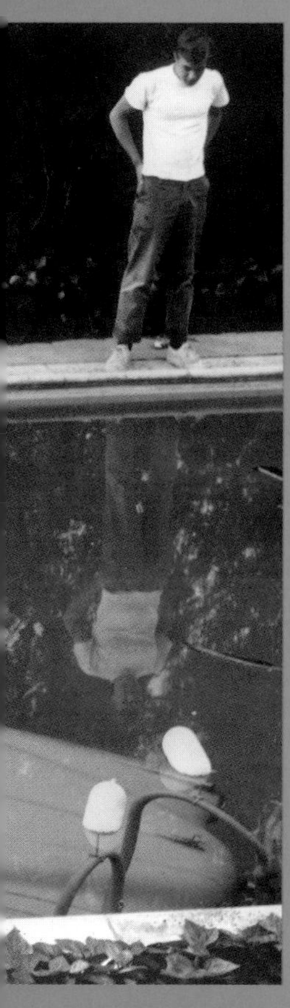

Doing easily what others find difficult is talent; doing what is impossible for talent is genius.

Henri-Frèdèric Amiel

Humor is mankind's greatest blessing.

Mark Twain

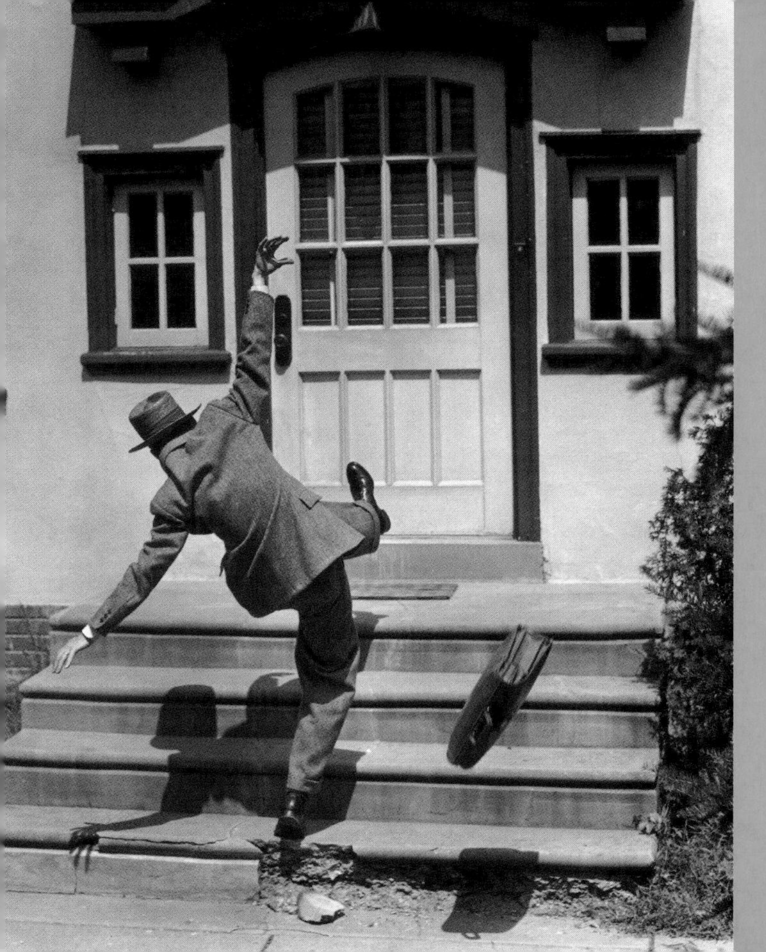

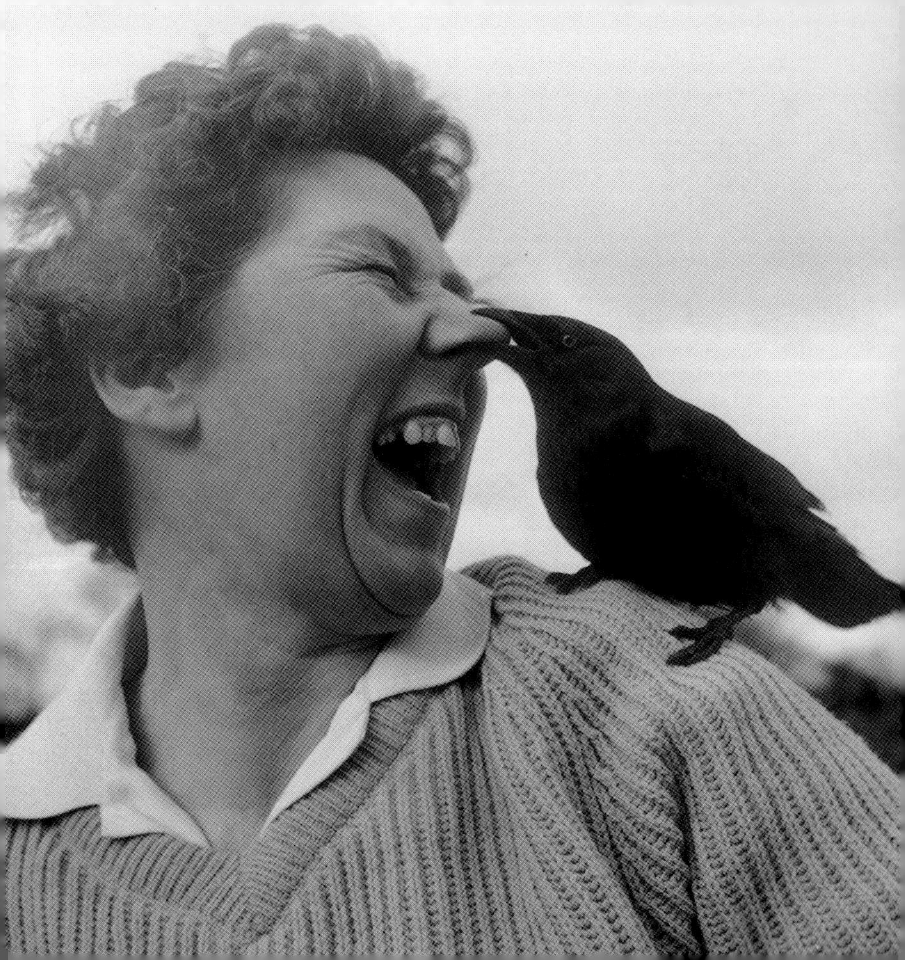

...The maid was in the garden,

Hanging out the clothes,

When down came a blackbird

And pecked off her nose.

Traditional nursery rhyme

If everyone is thinking alike

then somebody isn't thinking.

General George S. Patton

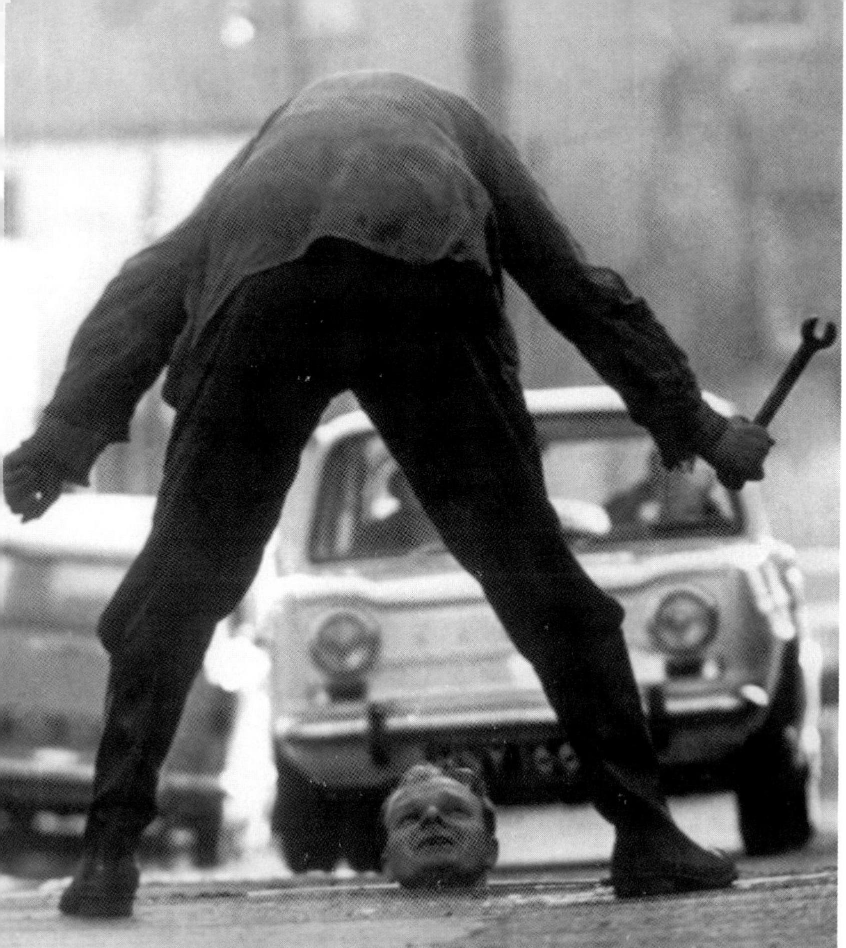

One's mind has a way of making itself up in the background, and it suddenly becomes clear what one means to do.

A.C. Benson

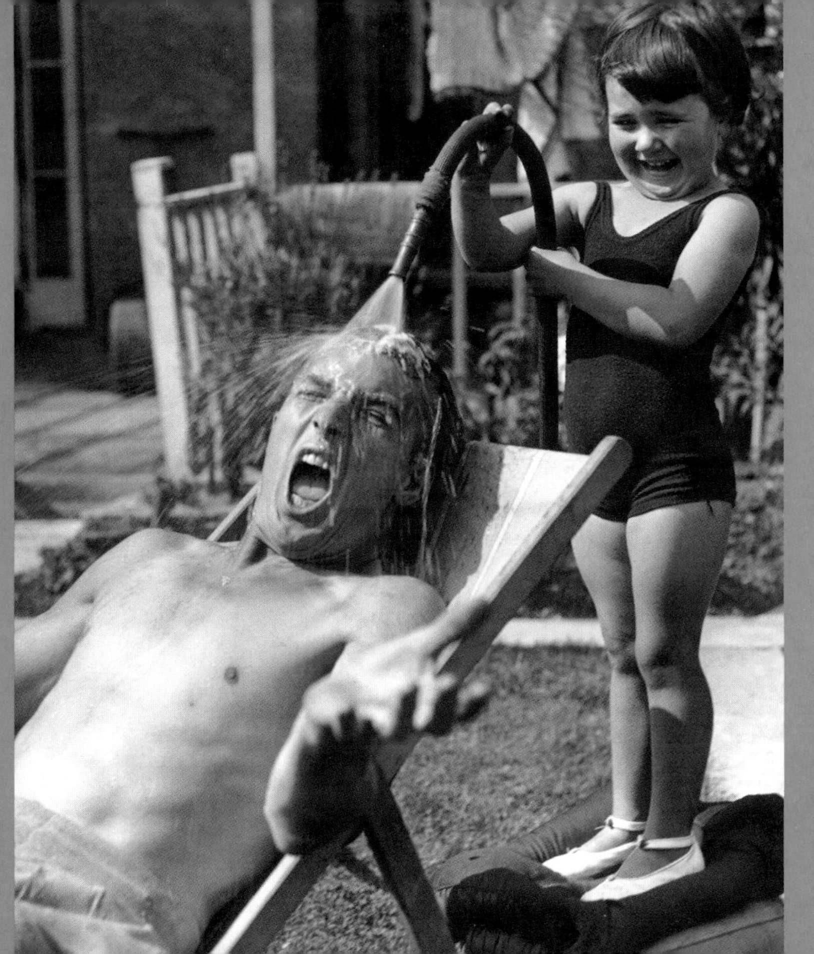

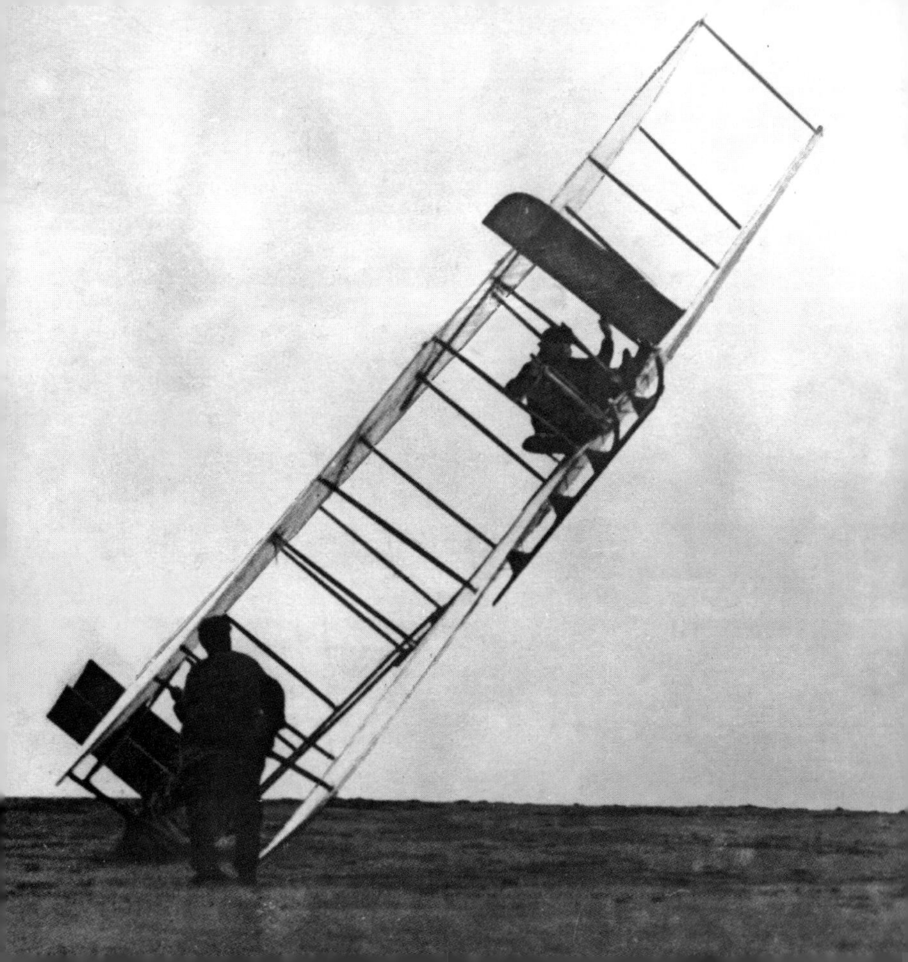

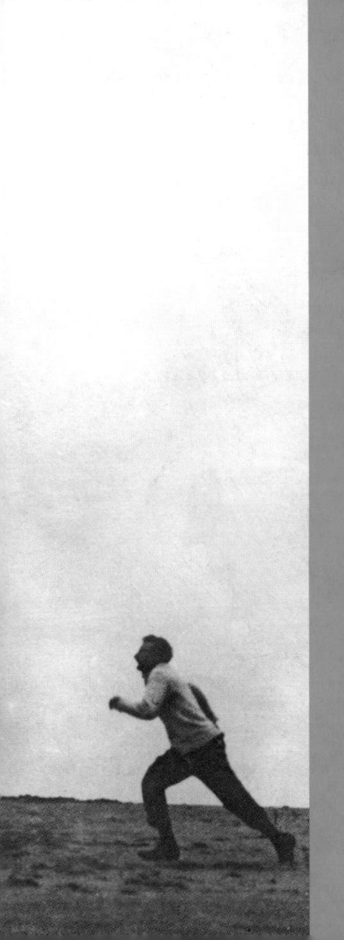

There lurks in every human heart a desire of distinction, which inclines every man first to hope, and then to believe, that Nature has given him something peculiar to himself.

Samuel Johnson

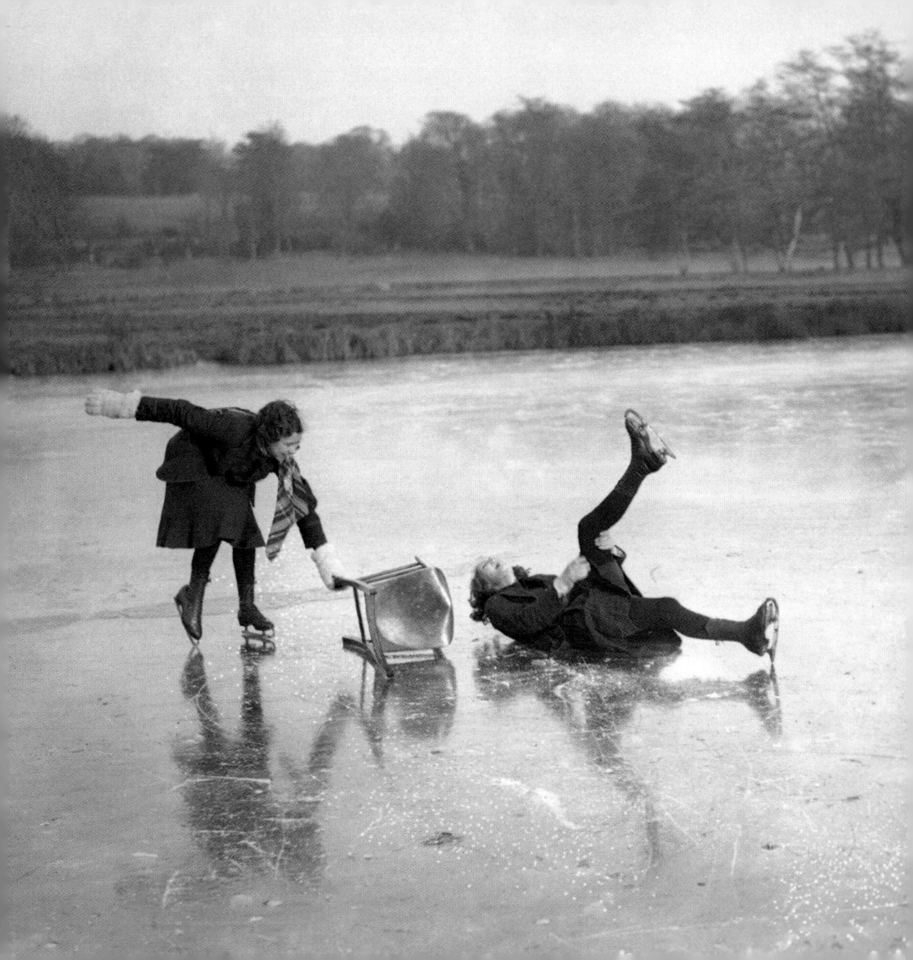

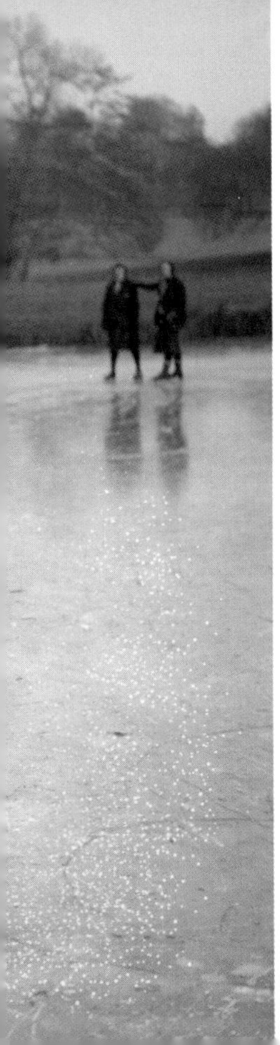

A life spent making mistakes

is not only more honorable

but more useful than a life

spent doing nothing.

George Bernard Shaw

Never, never, never, never

give up.

Winston Churchill

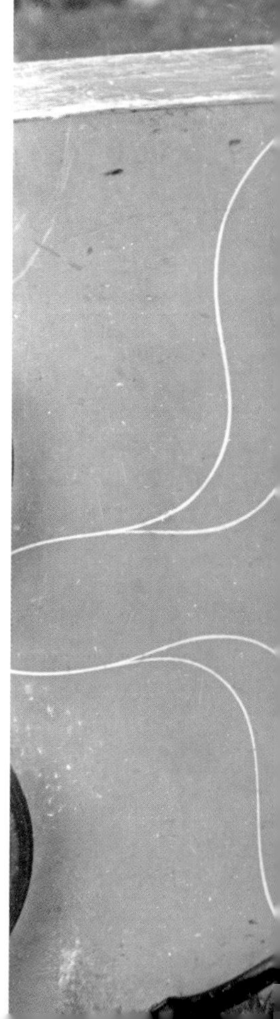

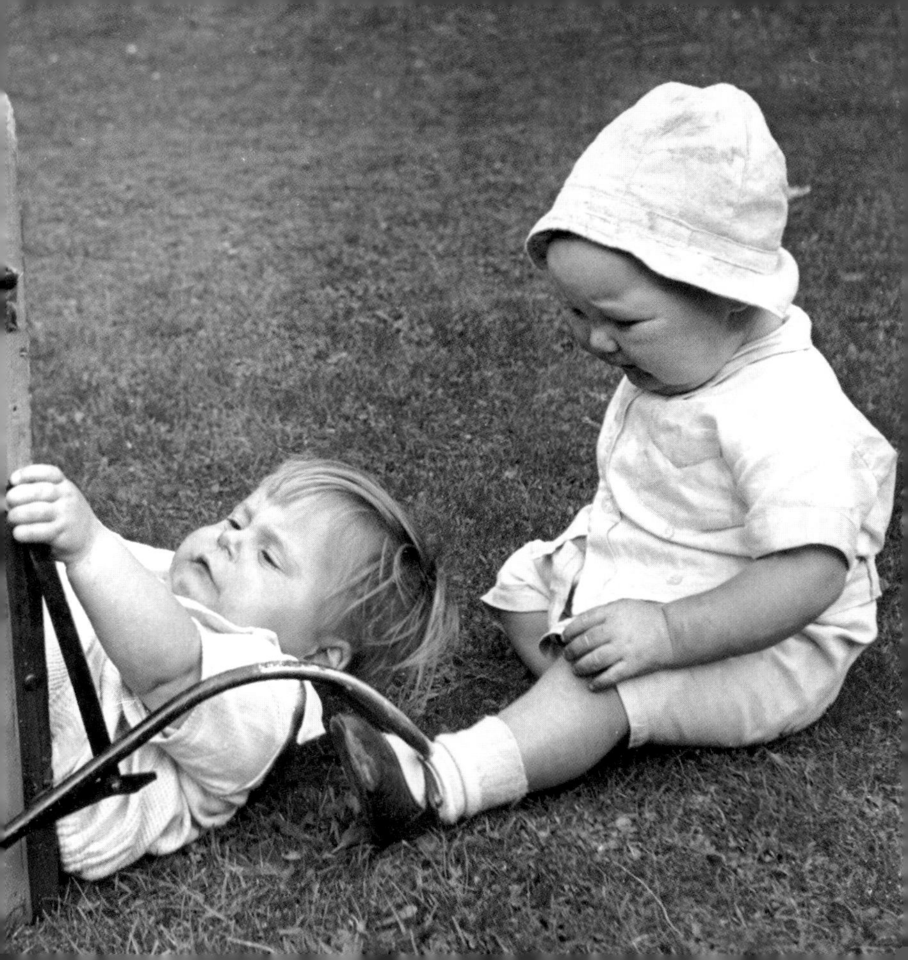

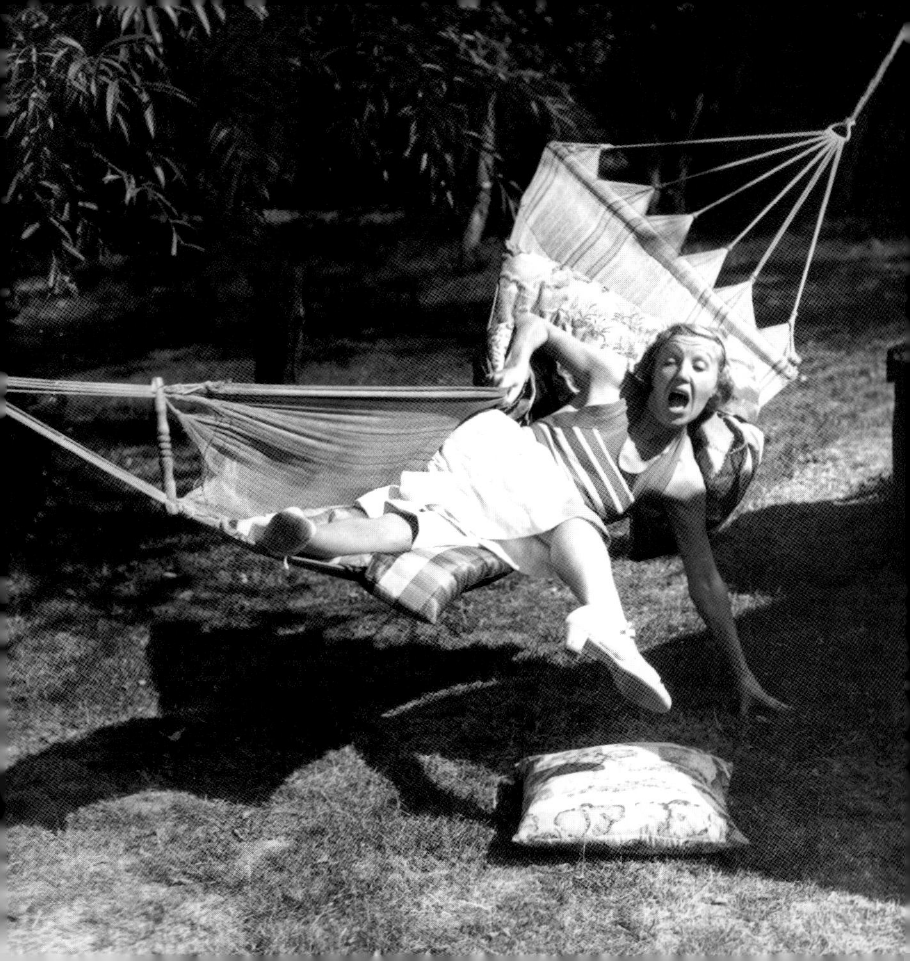

I am not concerned that you have fallen—I am concerned that you arise.

Abraham Lincoln

Most of the important things in the world have been accomplished by people who have kept on trying when there seemed to be no hope at all.

Dale Carnegie

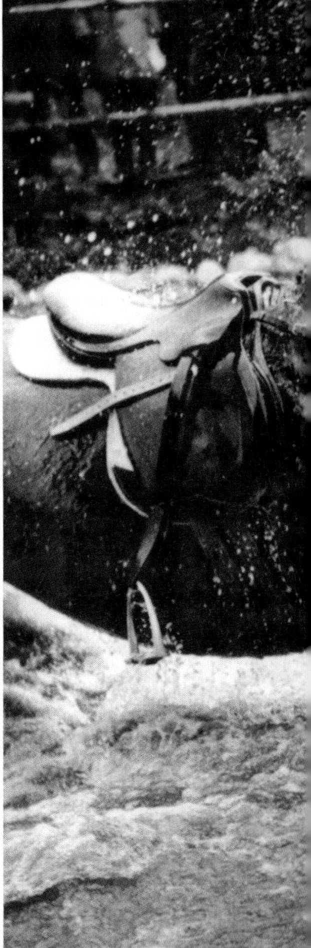

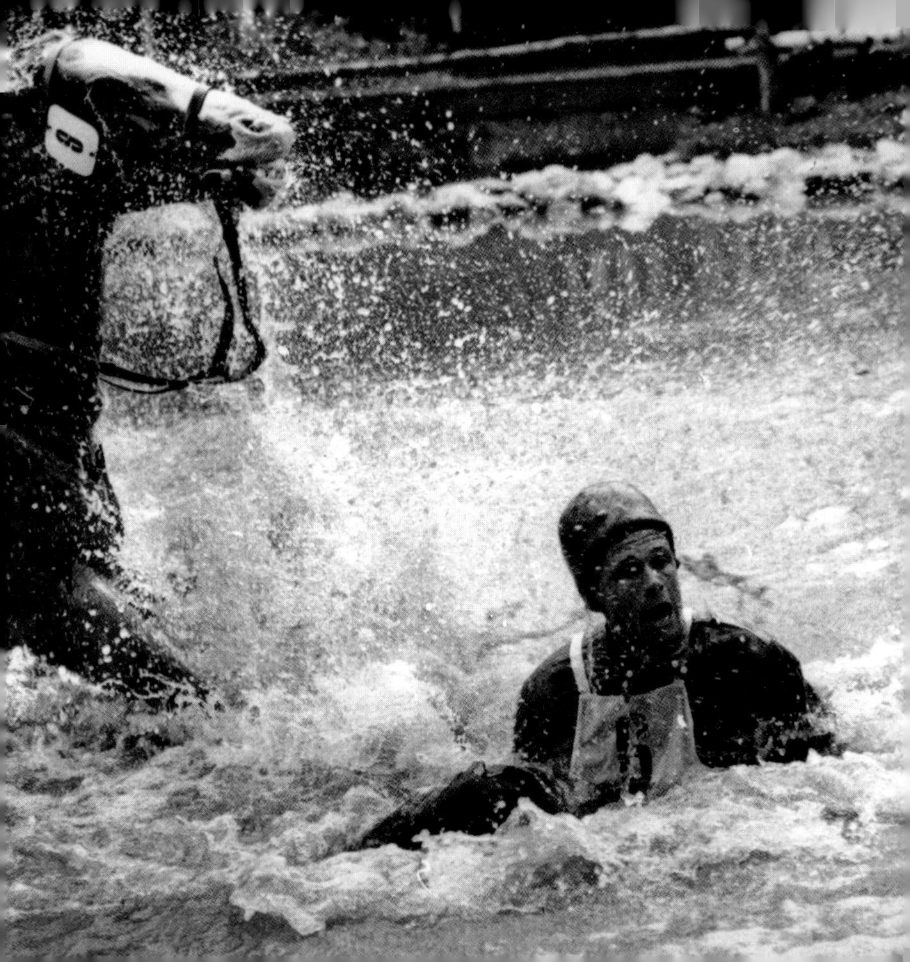

That is the best—to laugh with someone

because you both think the same things are funny.

Gloria Vanderbilt

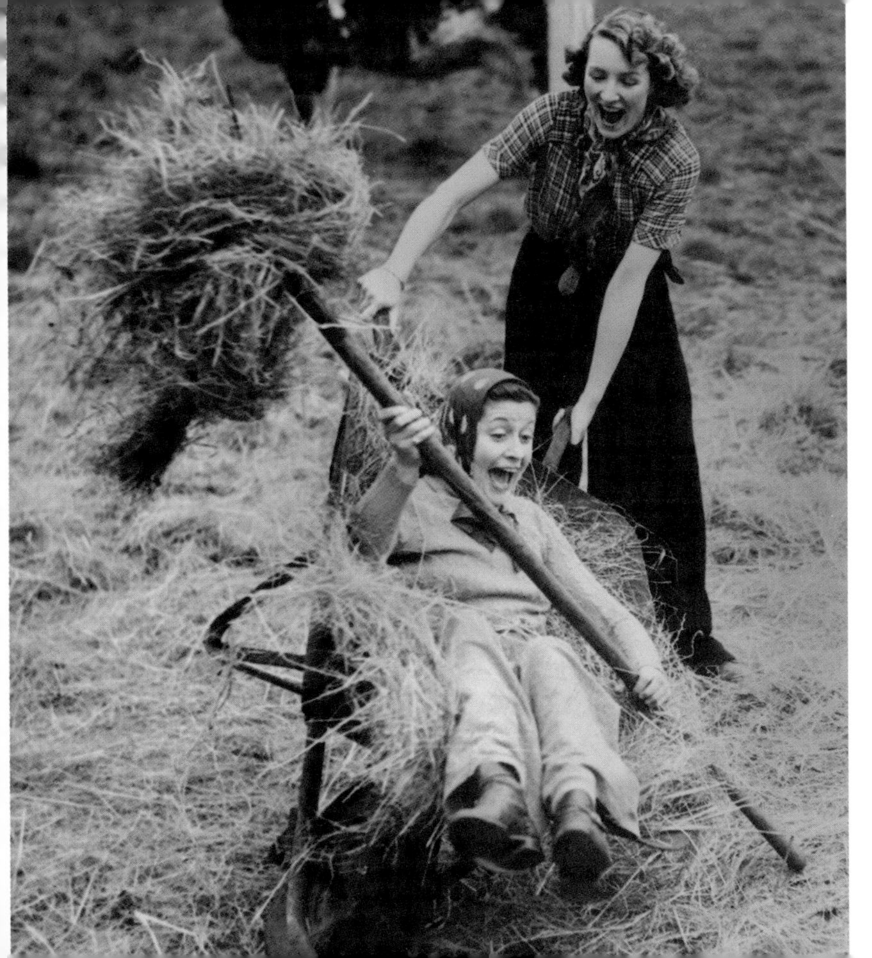

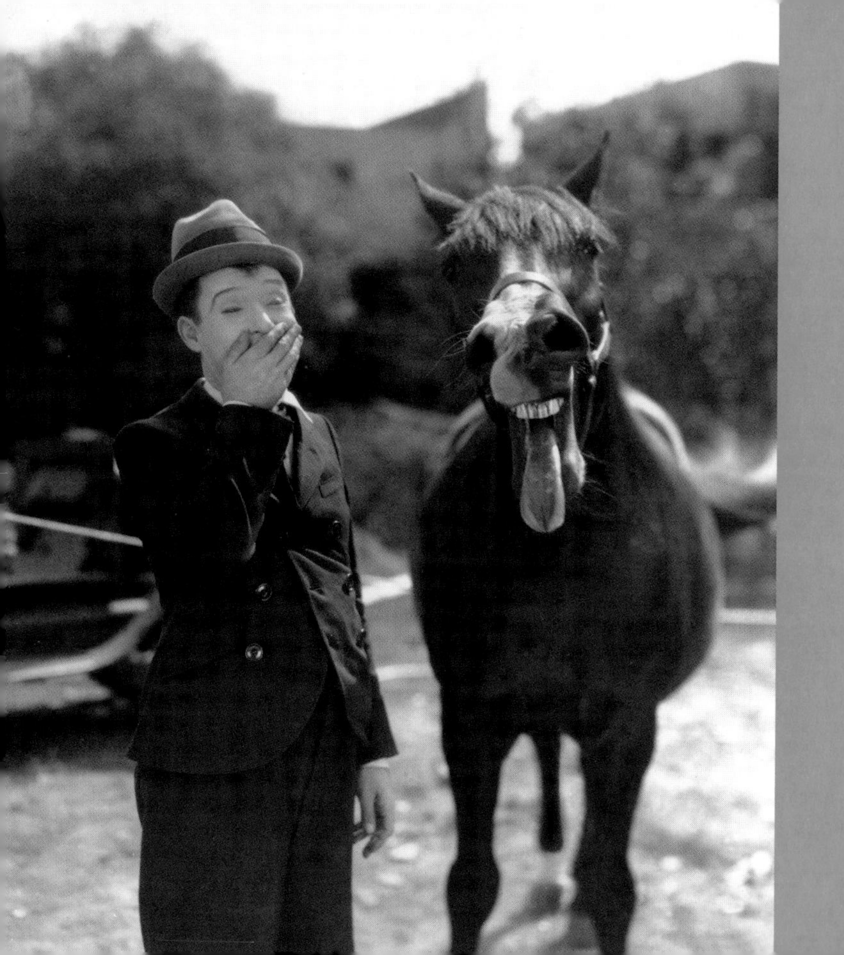

But the fact that some geniuses were laughed at does not imply that all who are laughed at are geniuses. They laughed at Columbus, they laughed at Fulton, they laughed at the Wright brothers. But they also laughed at Bozo the Clown.

Carl Sagan

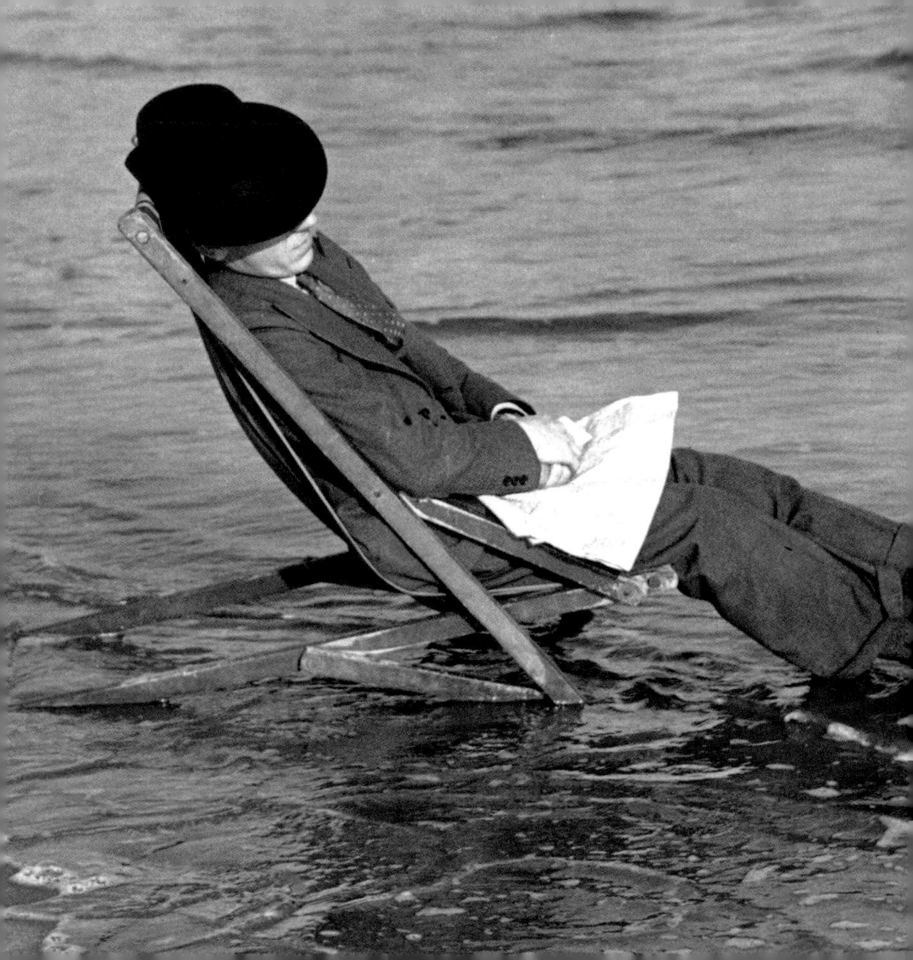

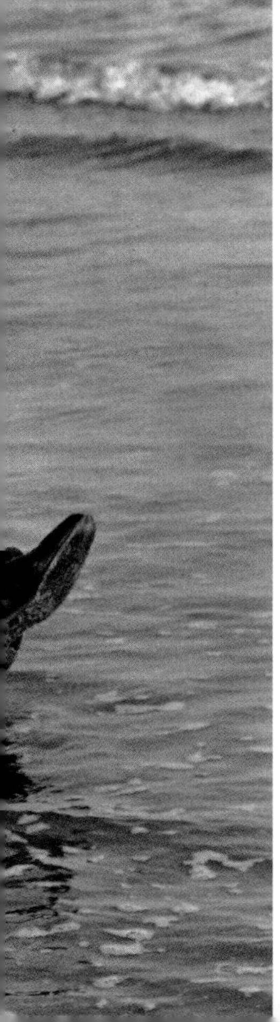

Every man of genius sees the world at a different angle from his fellows, and there is his tragedy.

Henry Havelock Ellis

More than any other time in history, mankind faces a crossroads. One path leads to despair and utter hopelessness. The other, to total extinction. Let us pray we have the wisdom to choose correctly.

Woody Allen speech

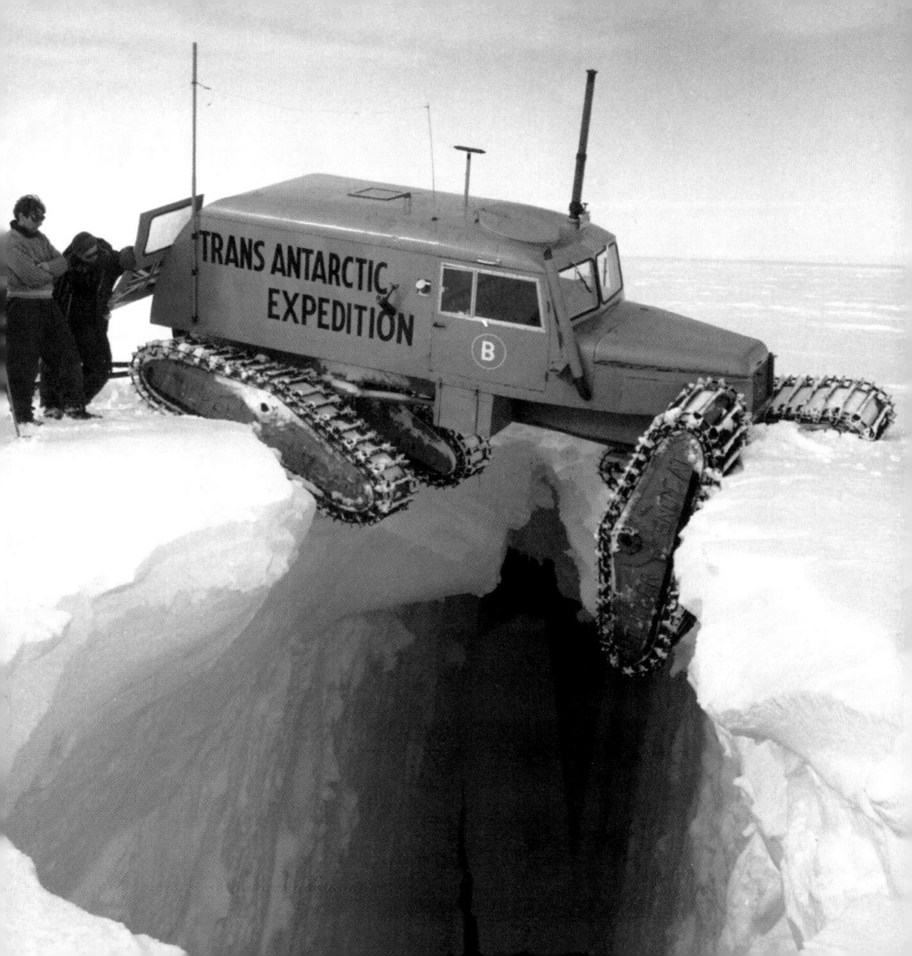
TRANS ANTARCTIC
EXPEDITION
B

Our plans miscarry because they have no aim. When a man does not know what harbor he is making for, no wind is the right wind.

Seneca

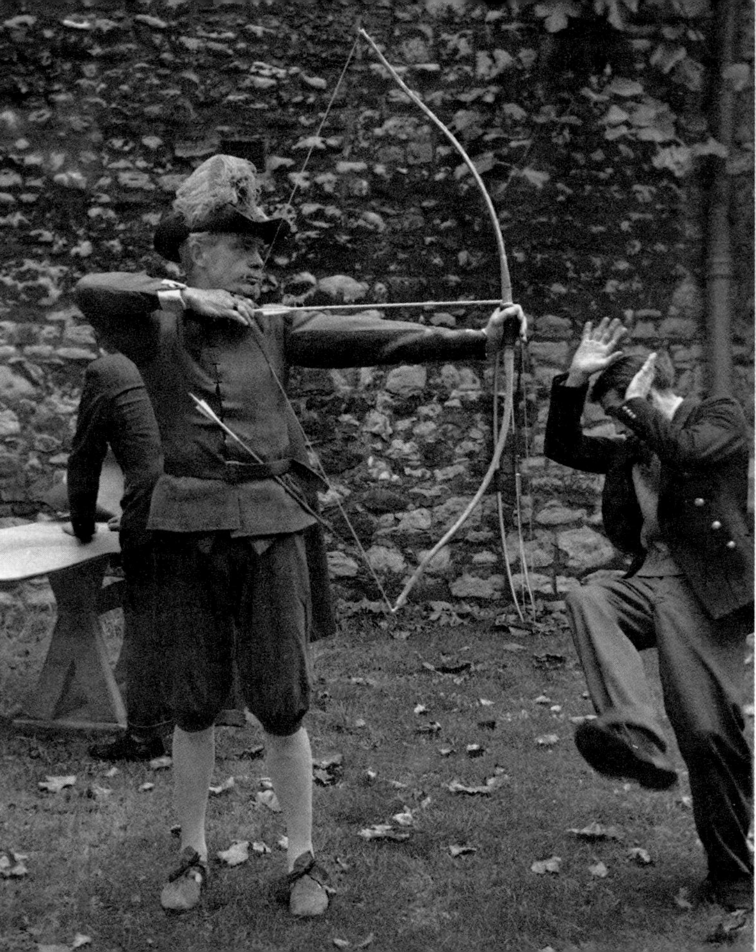

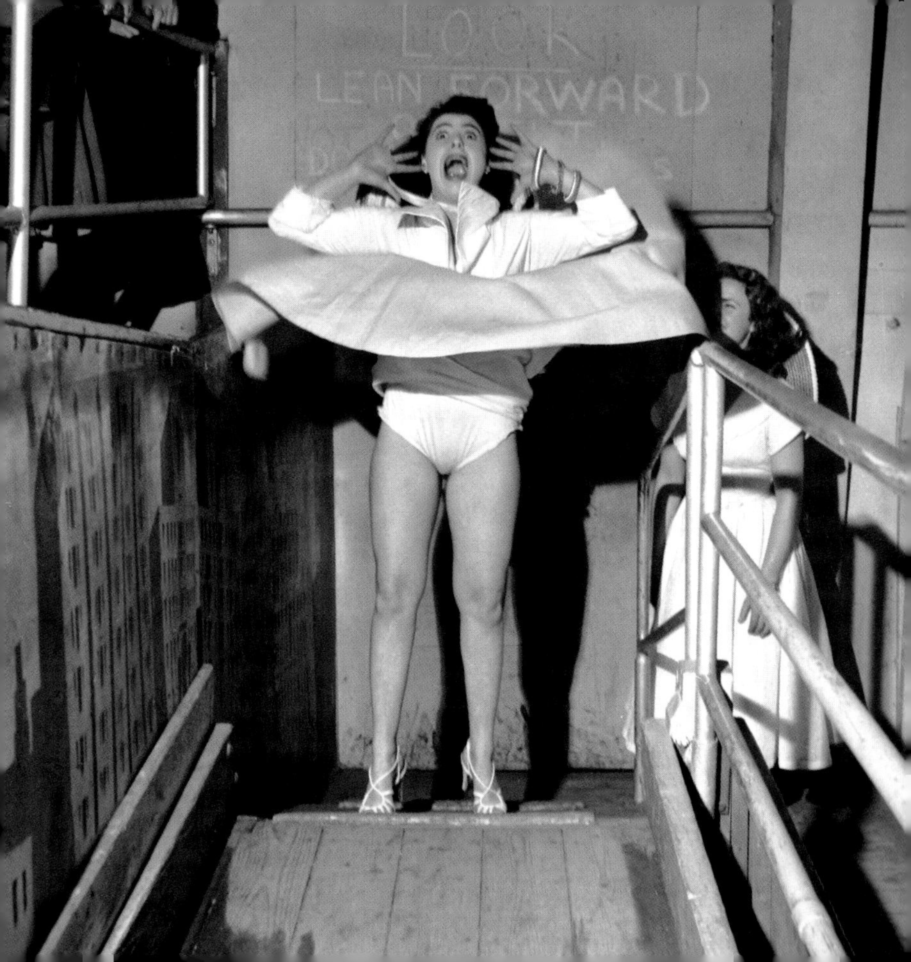
LOOK
LEAN FORWARD

Concealed talent brings no reputation.

Desiderius Erasmus

It is better to be beautiful than to be good. But...it is better to be good than to be ugly.

Oscar Wilde

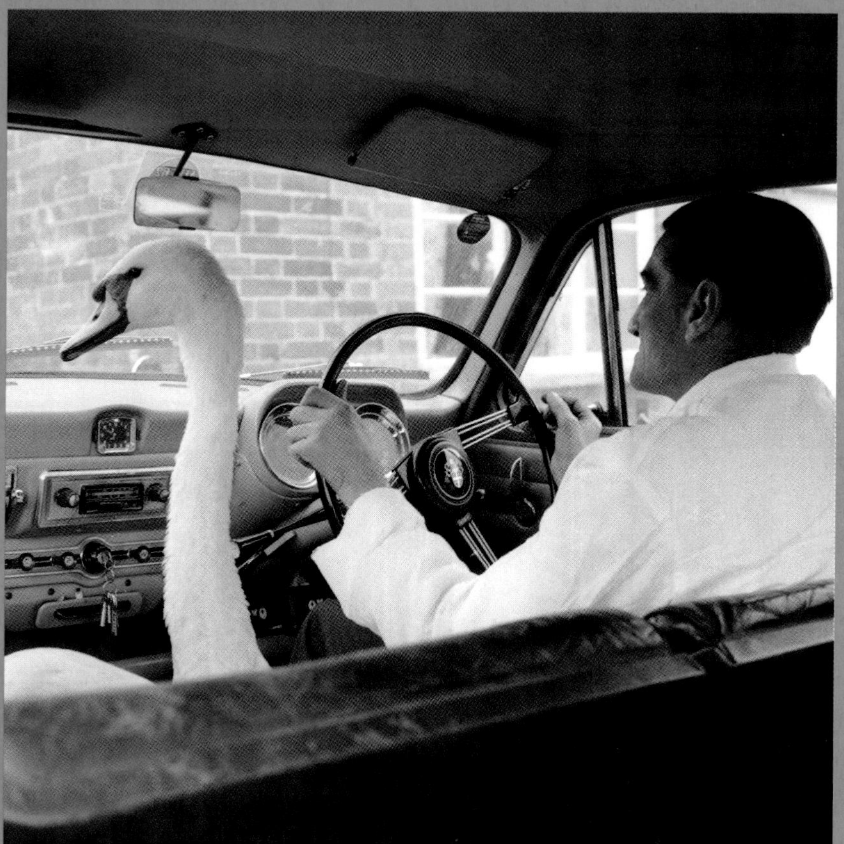

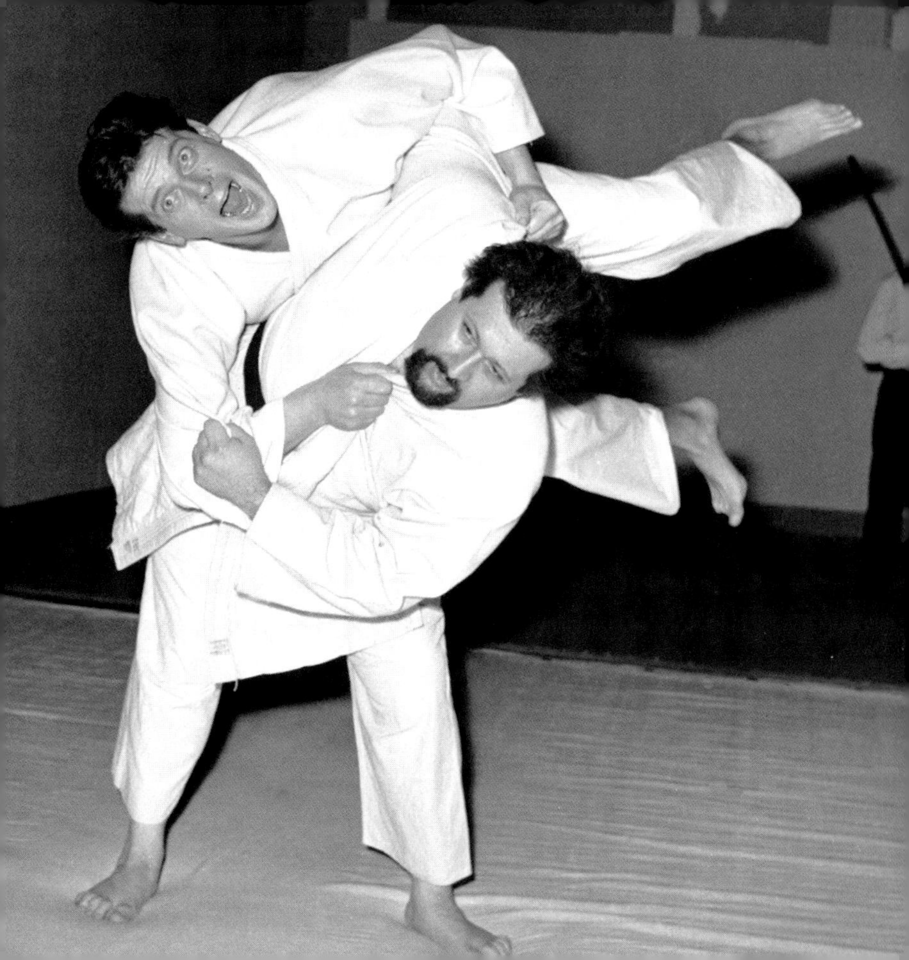

You become a champion by fighting one more round. When things are tough, you fight one more round.

James Corbett

If something anticipated arrives too late

it finds us numb, wrung out from waiting,

and we feel—nothing at all.

The best things arrive on time.

Dorothy Gilman

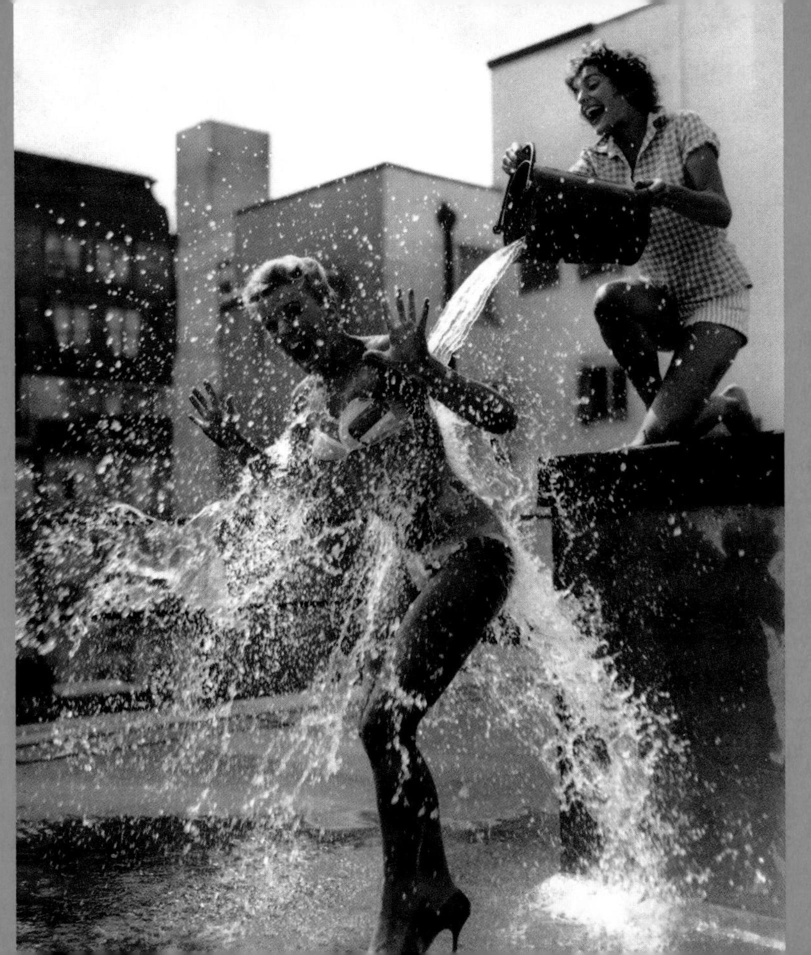

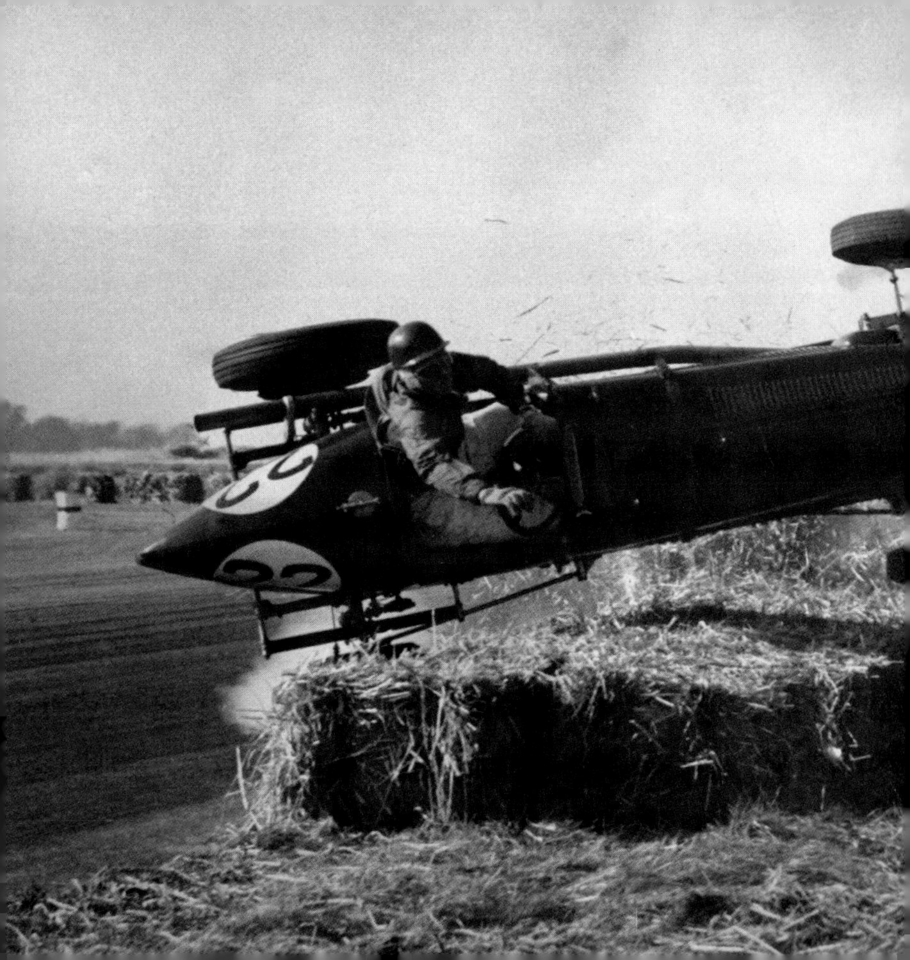

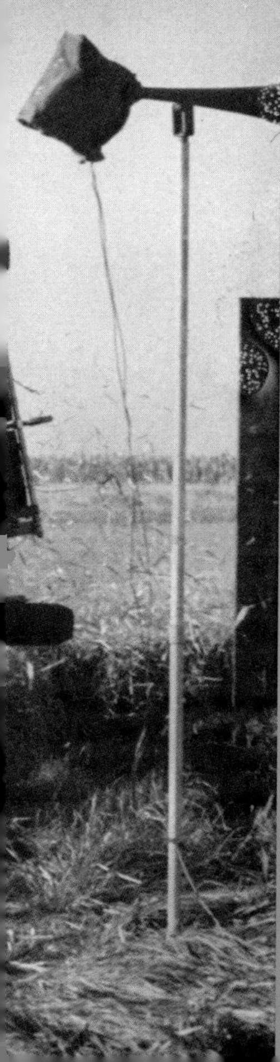

And while the law [of competition]
may be sometimes hard for the
individual, it is best for the race,
because it ensures the survival of
the fittest in every department.

Andrew Carnegie

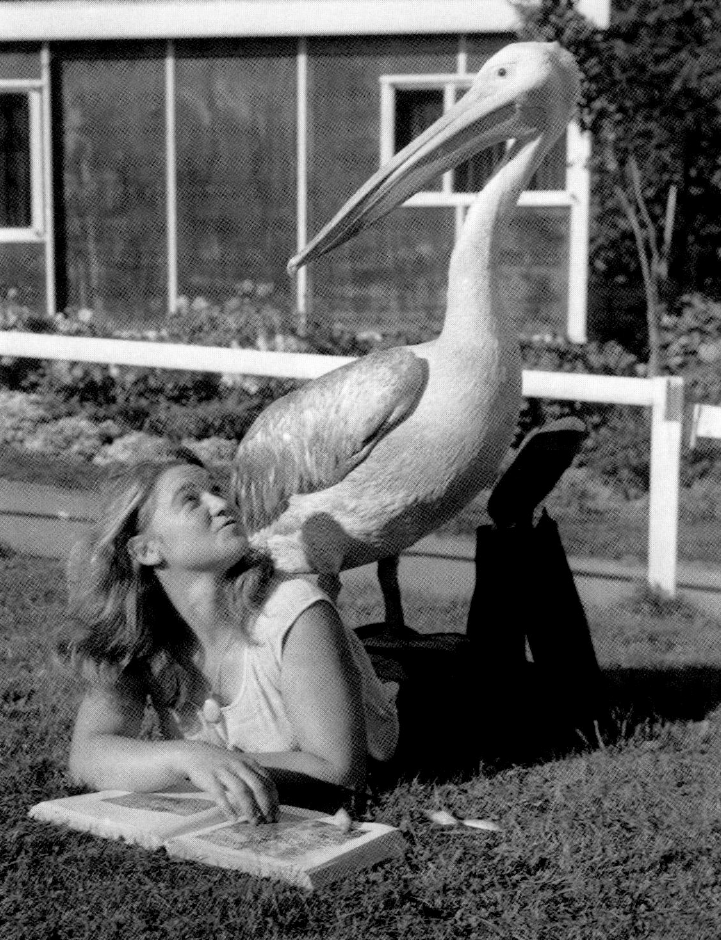

Somewhere, something incredible

is waiting to be known.

Carl Sagan

Genius is present in every age, but the men carrying it within them remain benumbed unless extraordinary events occur to heat up and melt the mass so that it flows forth.

Denis Diderot

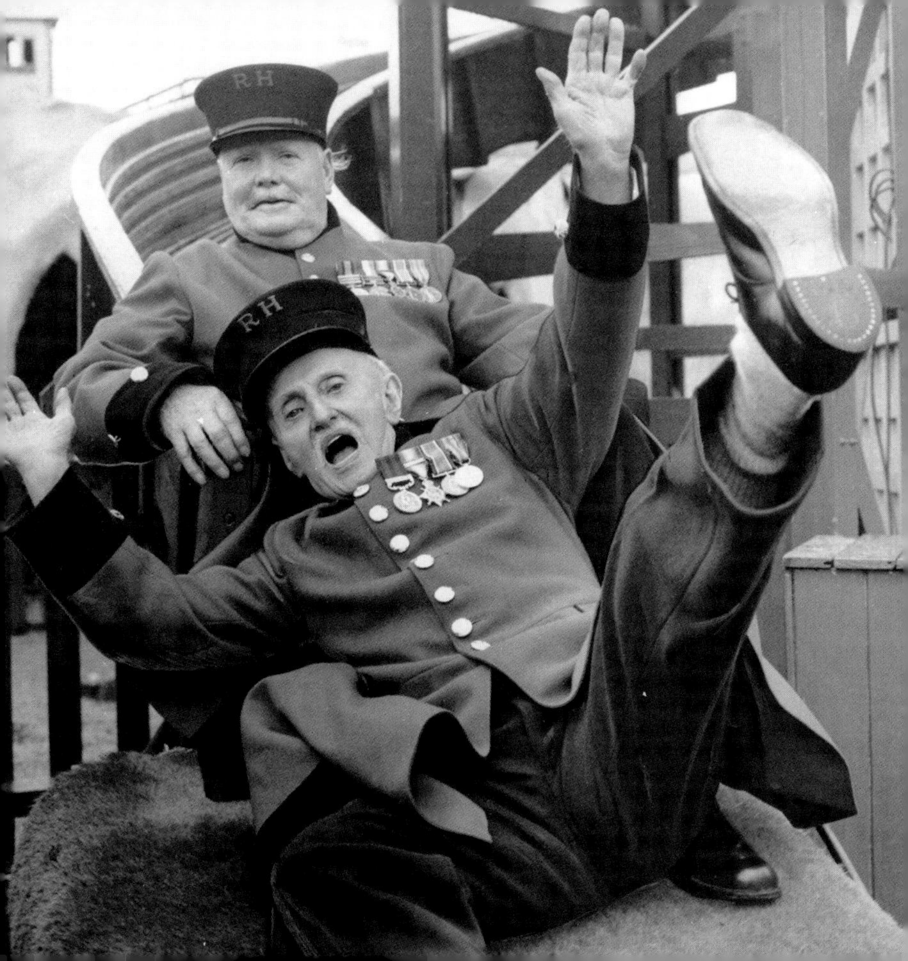
R H
R H

All of the animals
except man know that
the principle business
of life is to enjoy it.

Anonymous

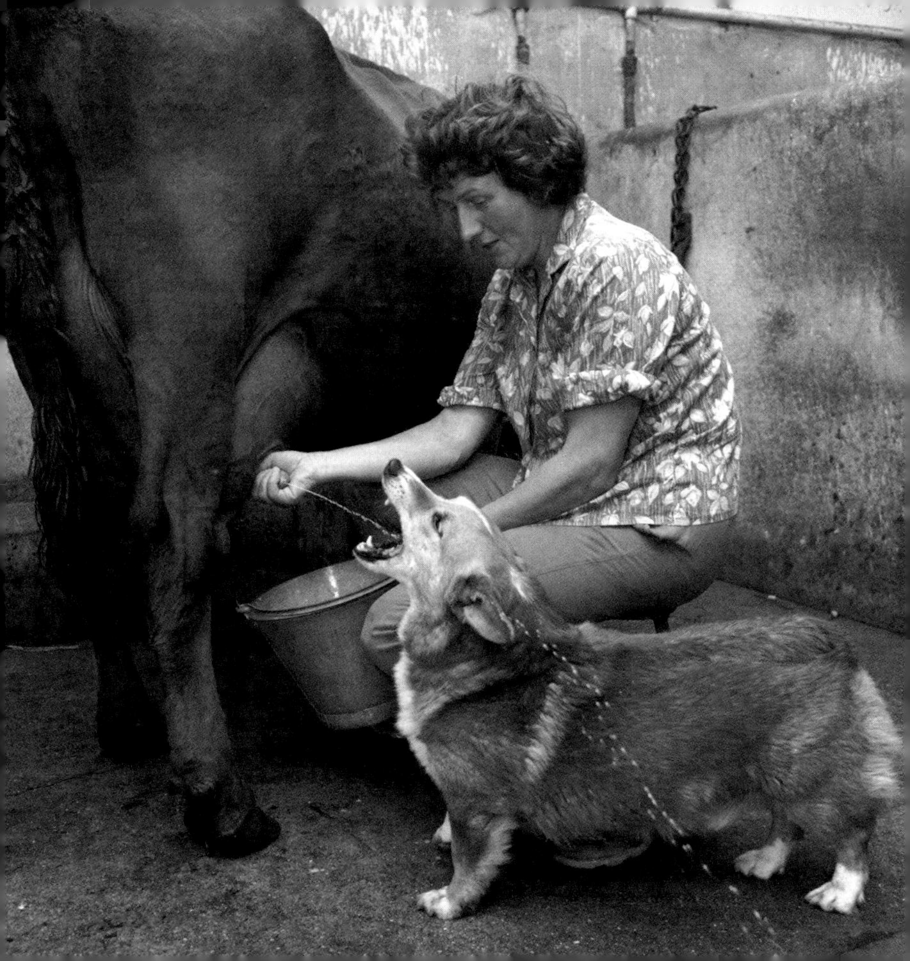

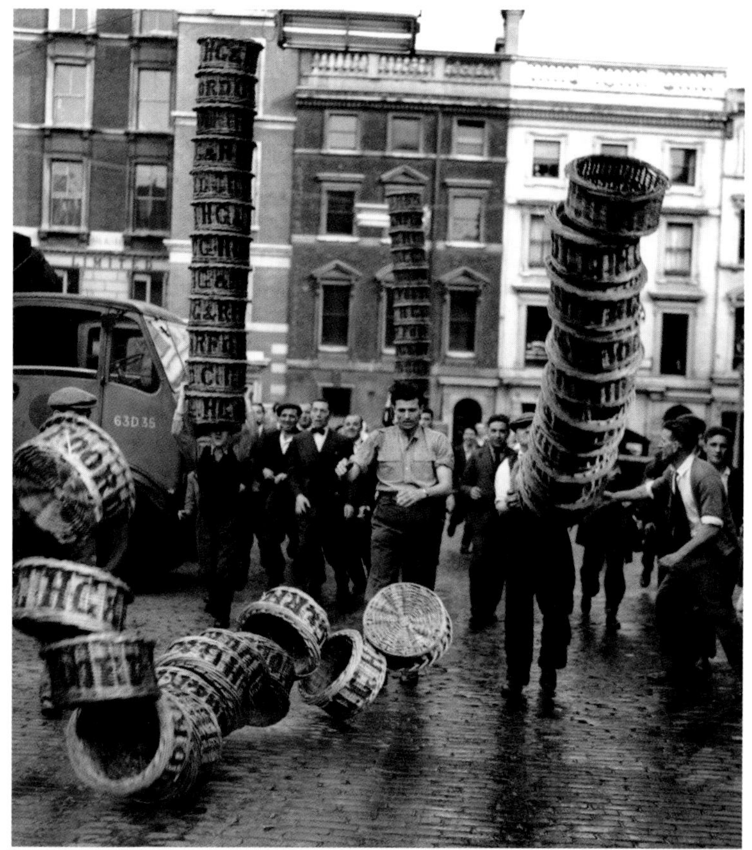
63D 35

Everything that is new or uncommon raises a pleasure in the imagination, because it fills the soul with an agreeable surprise, gratifies its curiosity, and gives it an idea of which it was not before possessed.

Joseph Addison

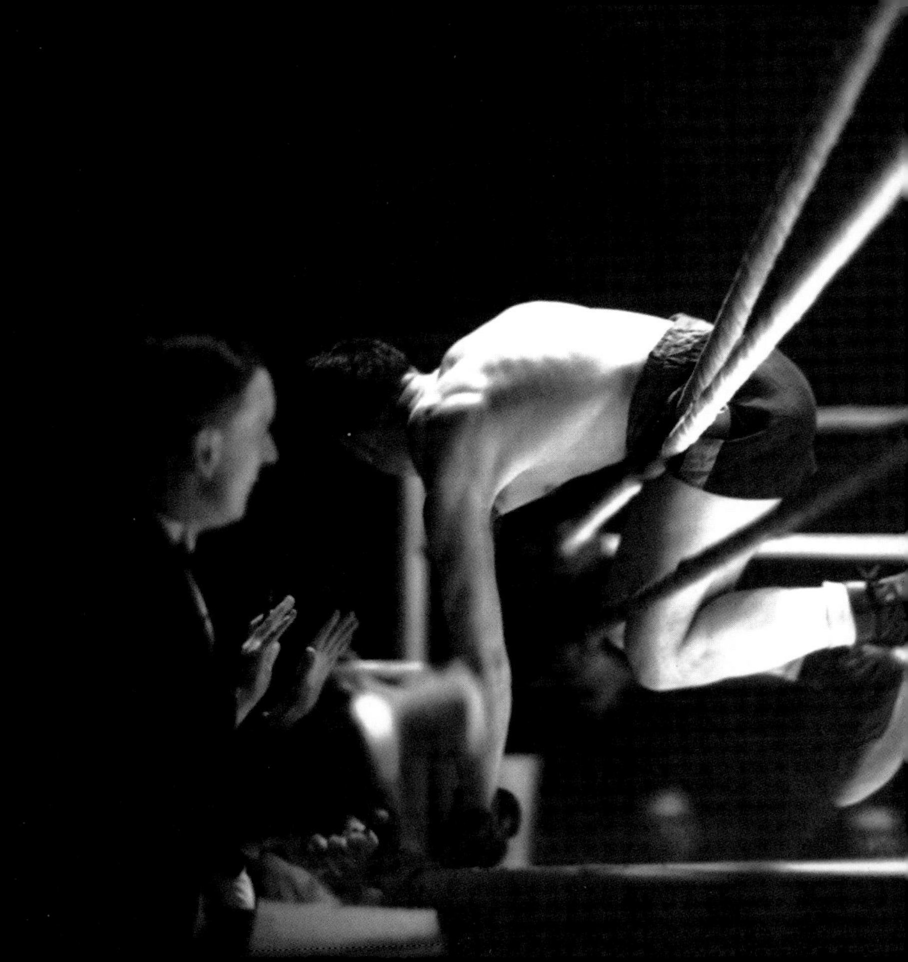

By three methods we may learn wisdom: First, by reflection, which is noblest; second, by imitation, which is easiest; and third by experience, which is the bitterest.

Confucius

Don't be afraid if things seem difficult in the beginning. That's only the initial impression. The important thing is not to retreat; you have to master yourself.

Olga Korbut

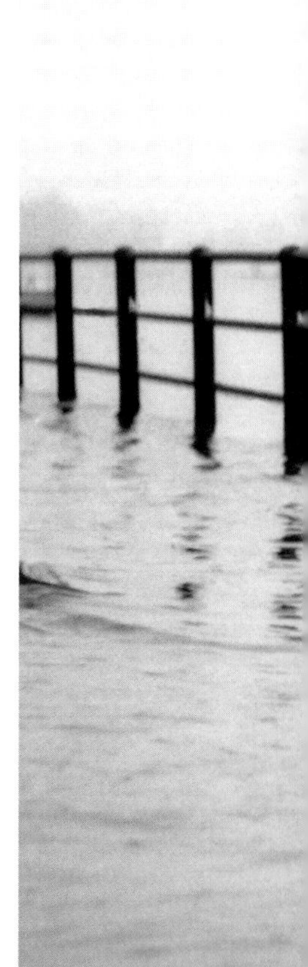

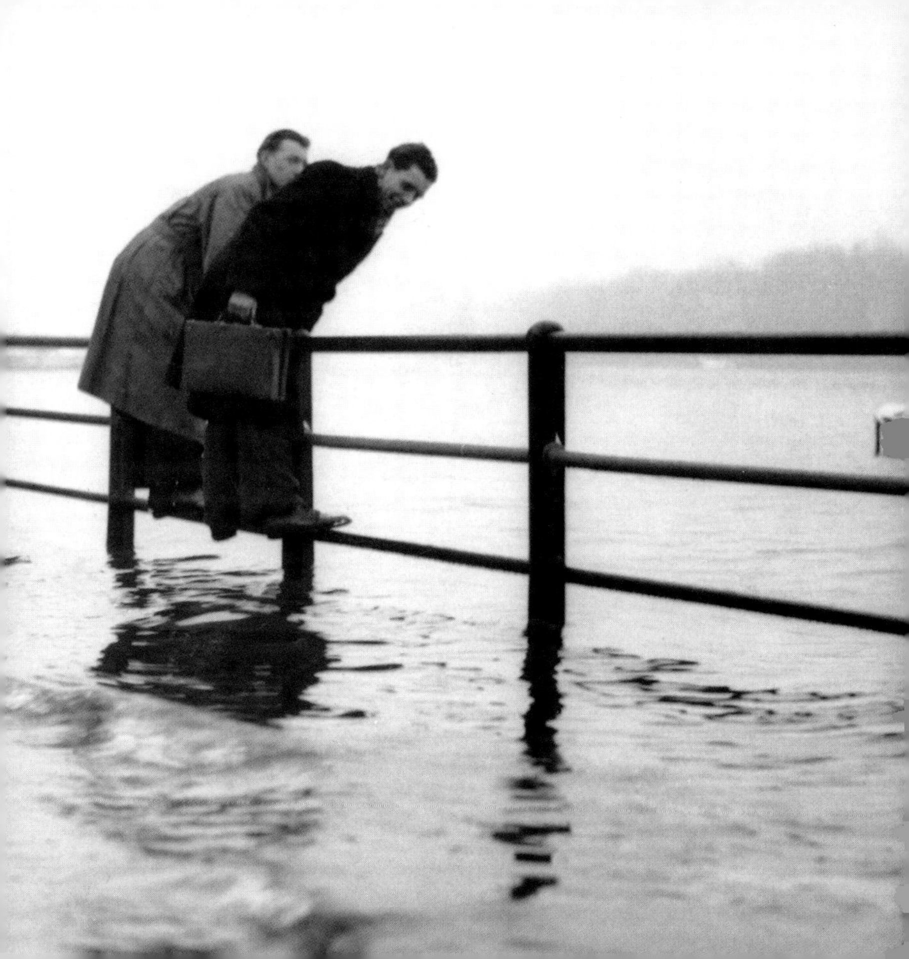

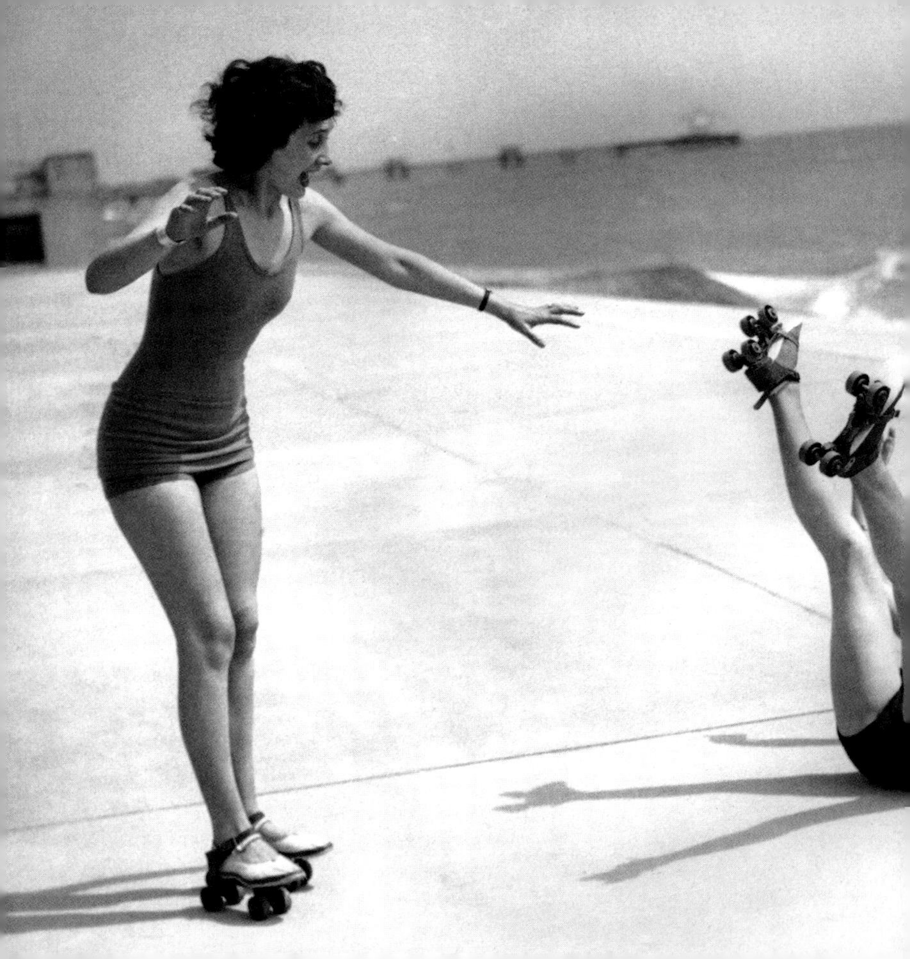

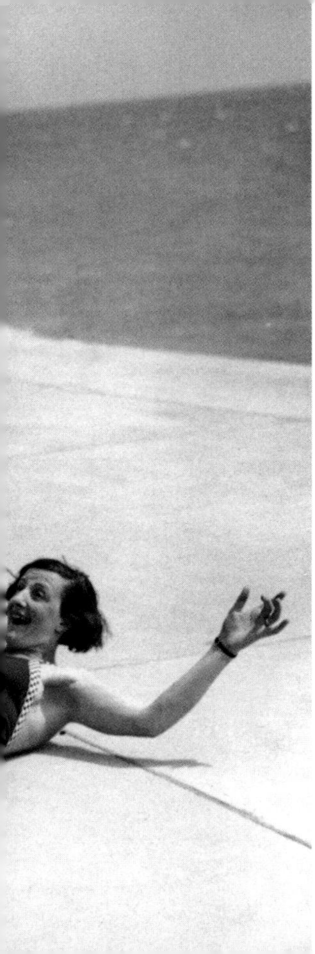

Talent is commonly developed at the expense of character.

Ralph Waldo Emerson

Patience is the

companion of wisdom.

Saint Augustine

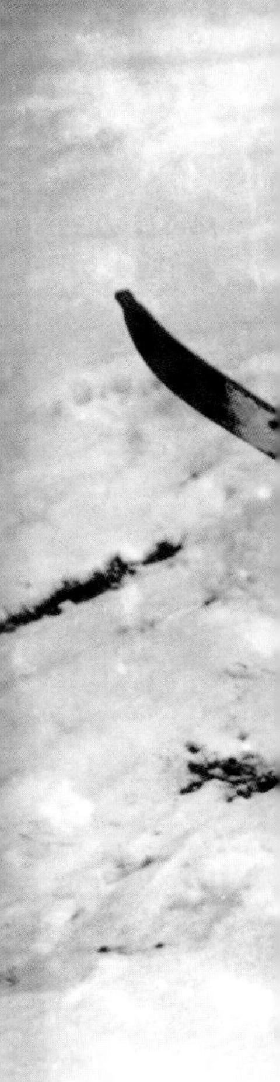

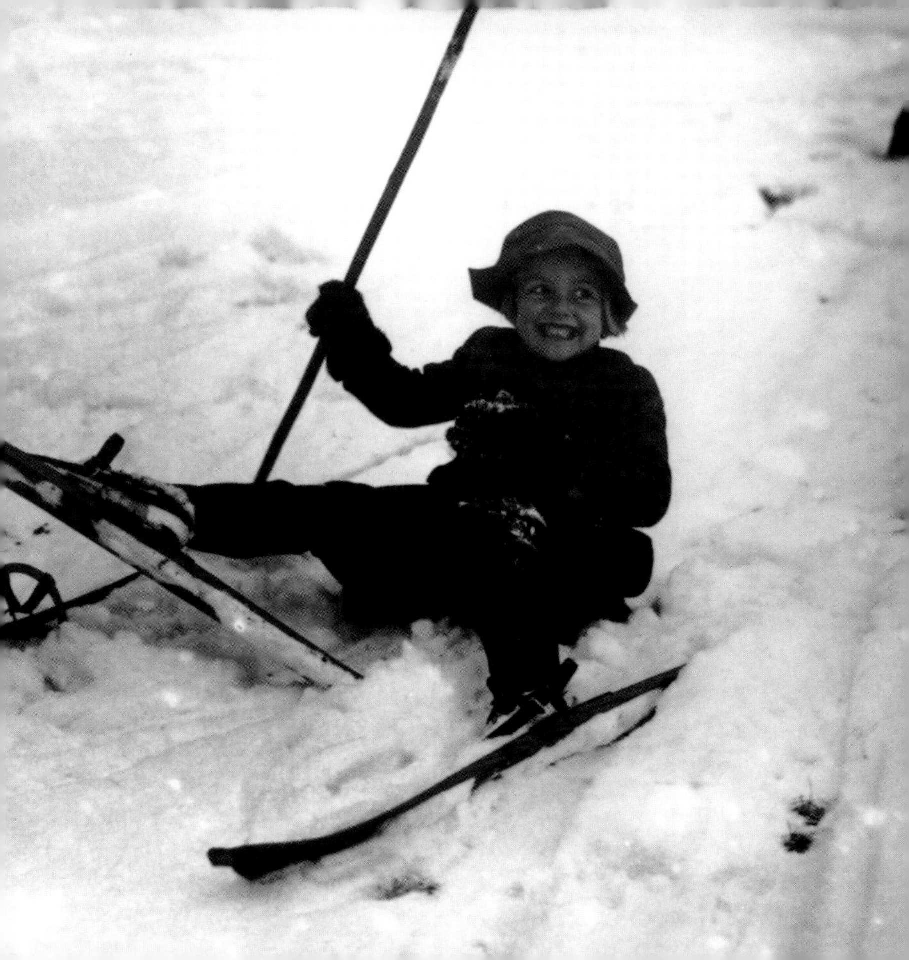

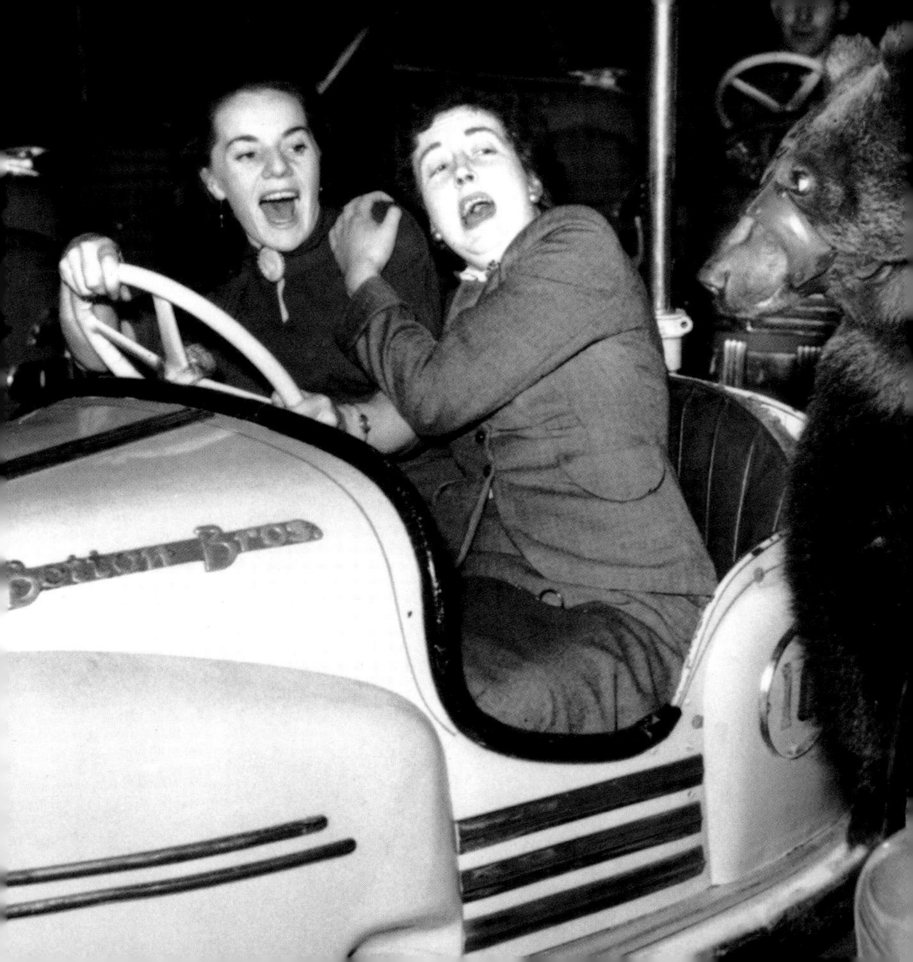

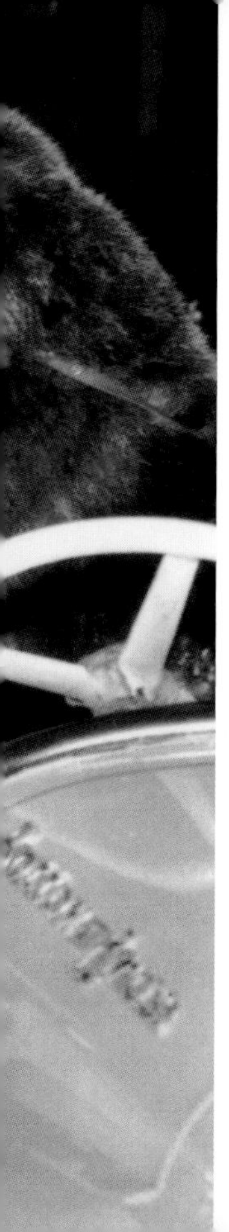

You can't really be strong

until you see a funny side to things.

Ken Kesey

Every man has his own vocation, talent is the call.

Ralph Waldo Emerson

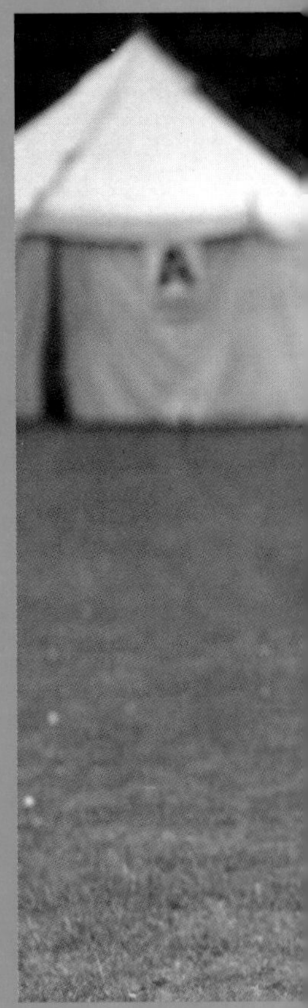

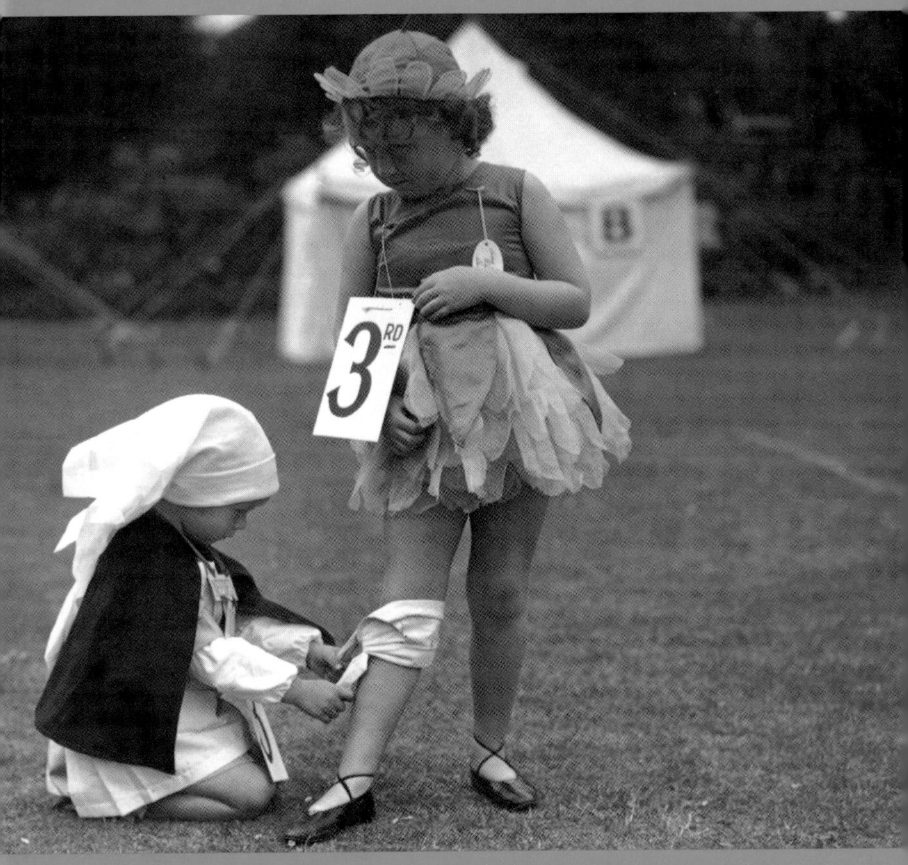
3RD

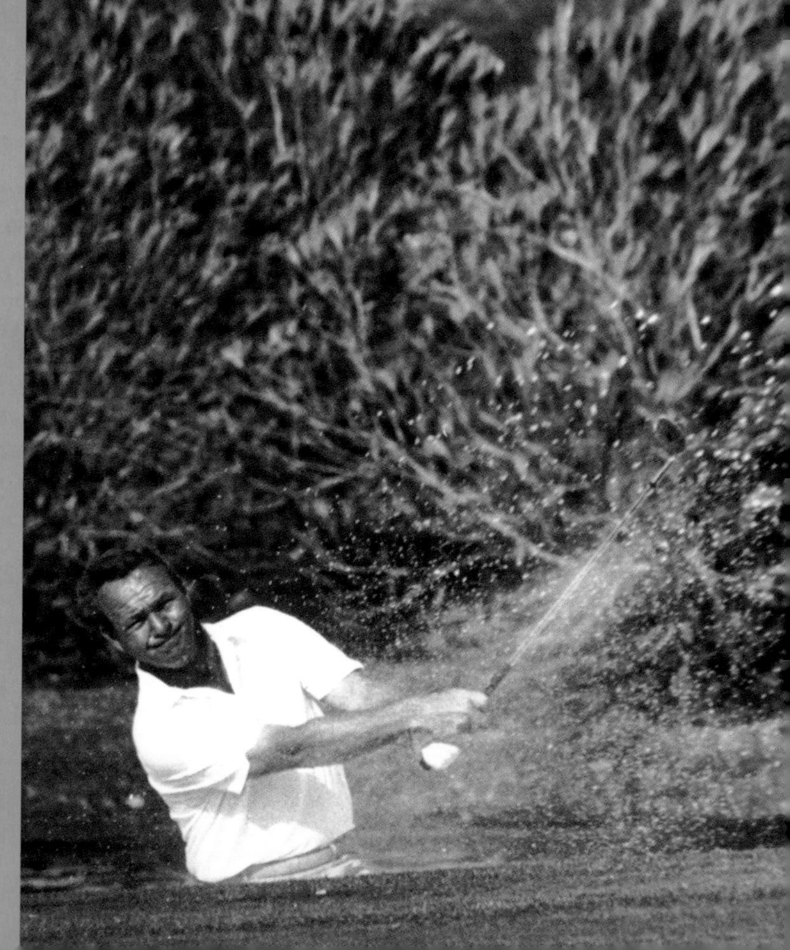

A man is not finished when he's defeated;

he's finished when he quits.

Richard M. Nixon

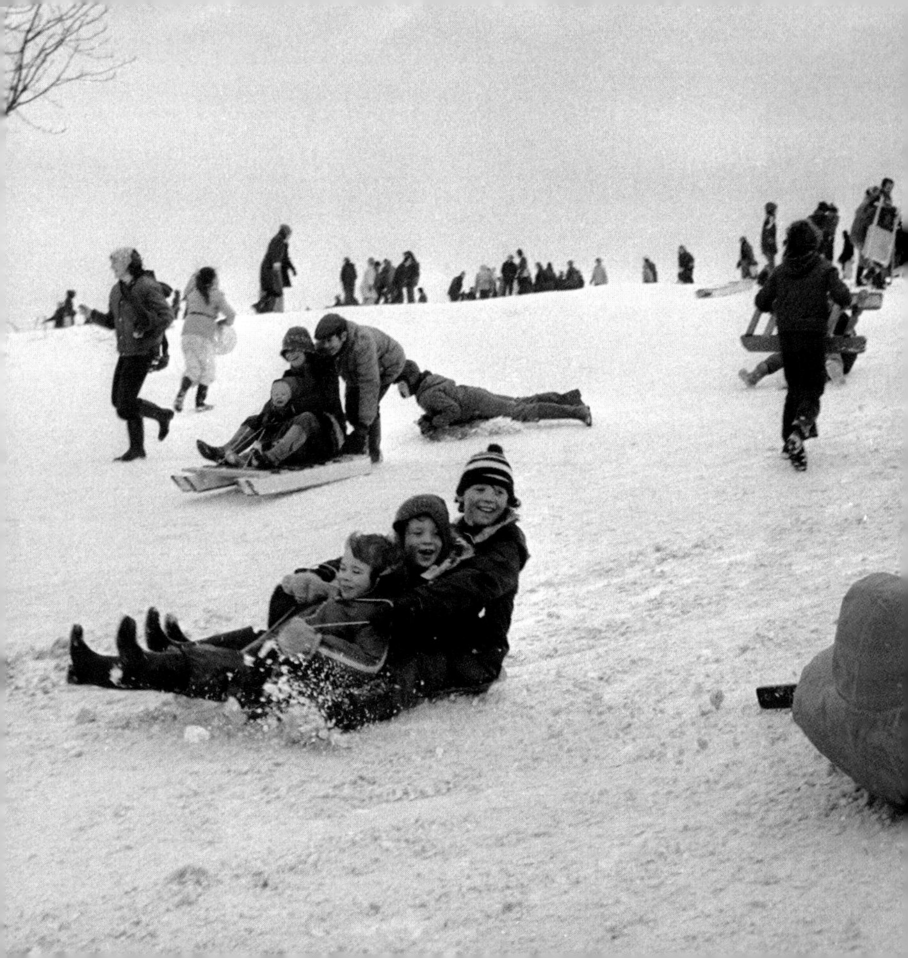

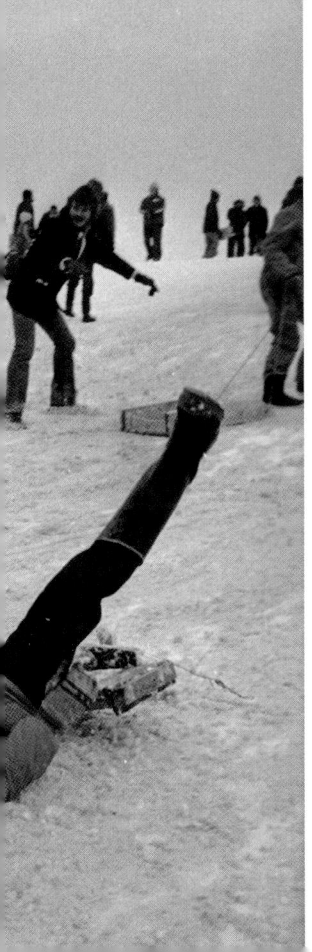

Every man has his follies—

and often they are the most

interesting thing he has got.

Josh Billings

Many of life's failures are people who did not realize how close they were to success when they gave up.

Thomas Edison

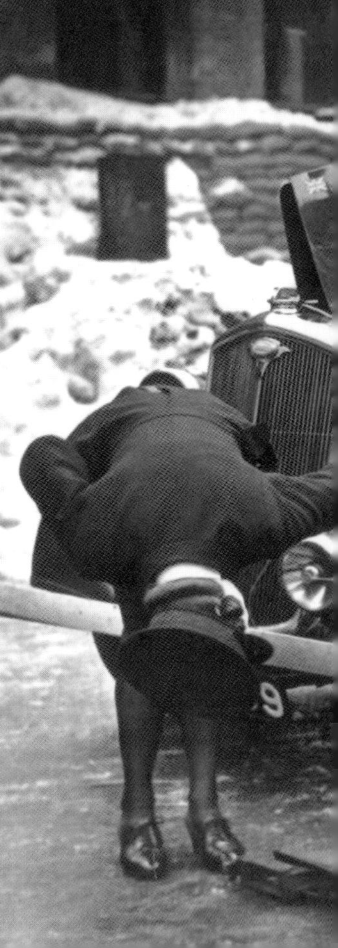

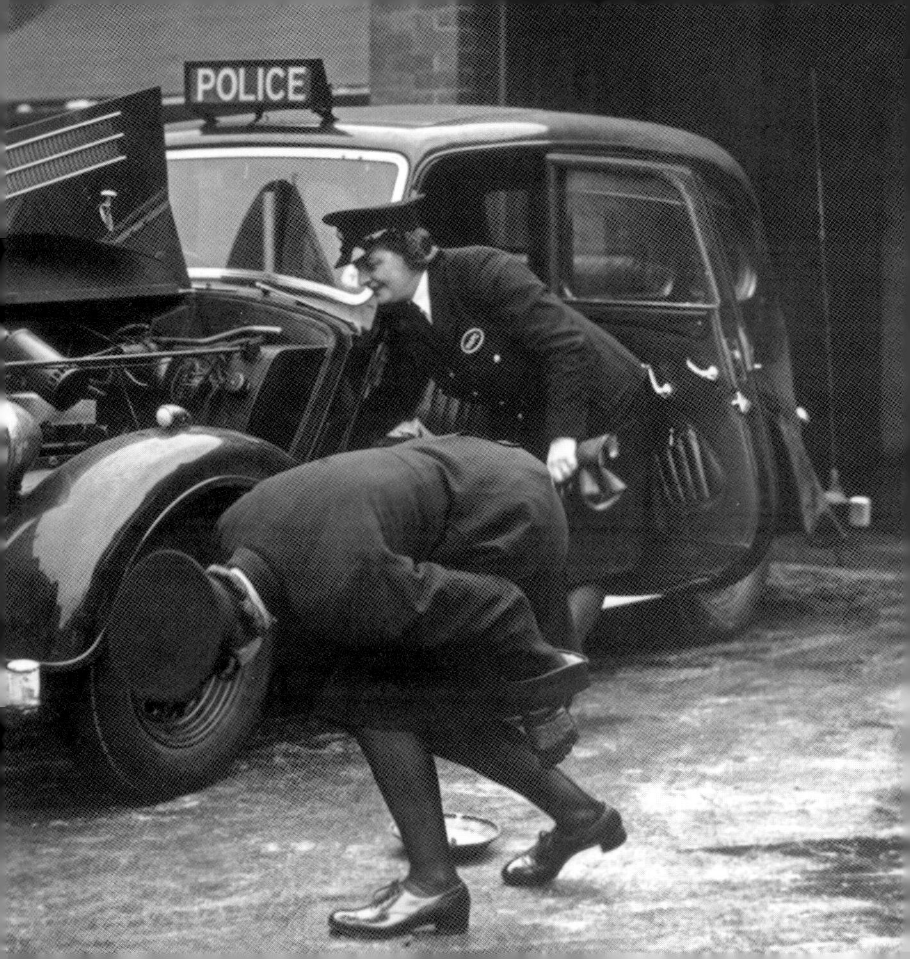
POLICE

There is a risk you cannot afford to take, and there is the risk you cannot afford not to take.

Peter Drucker

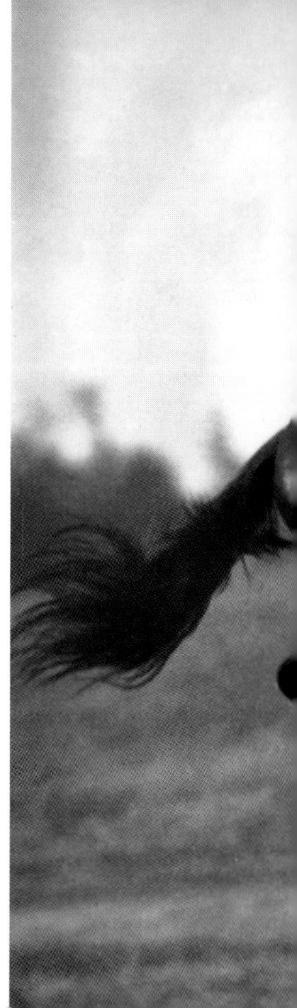

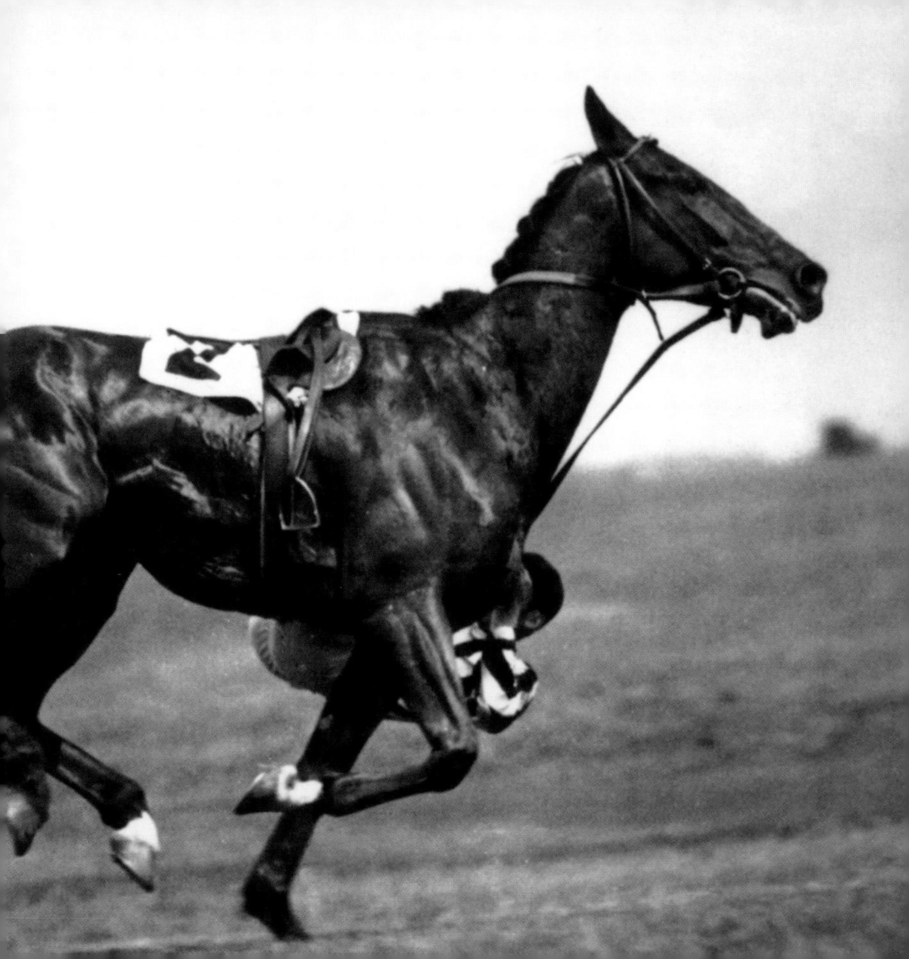

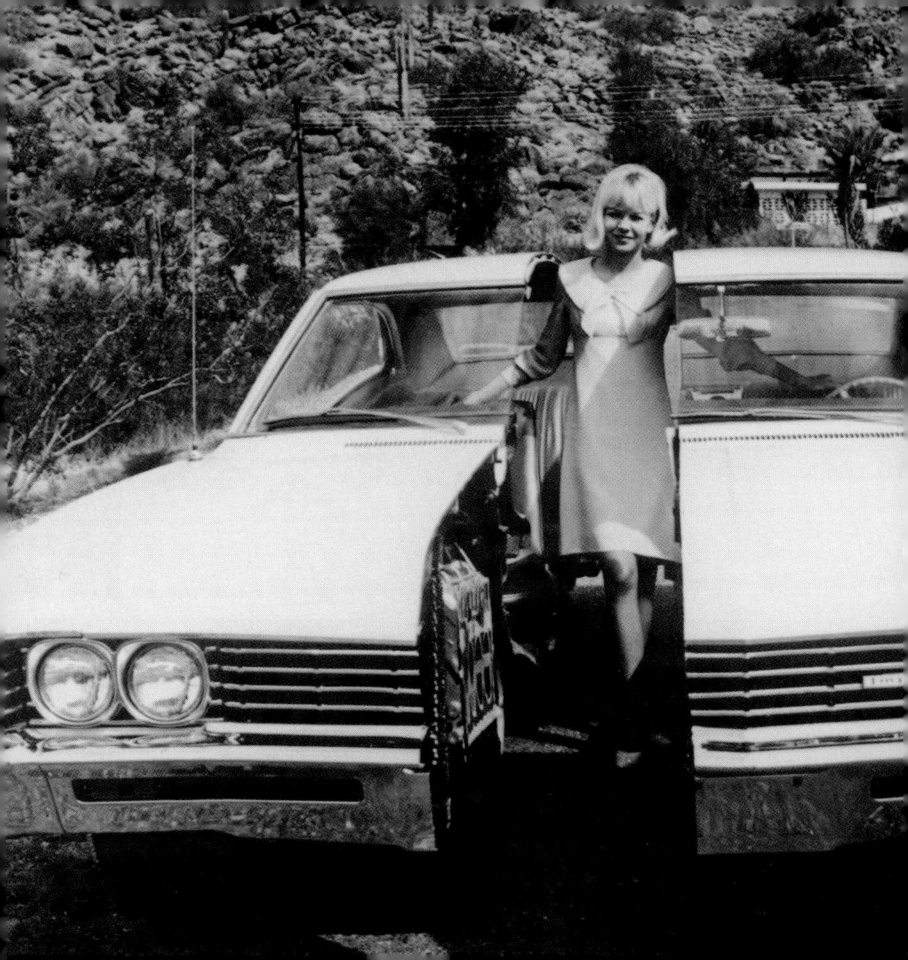

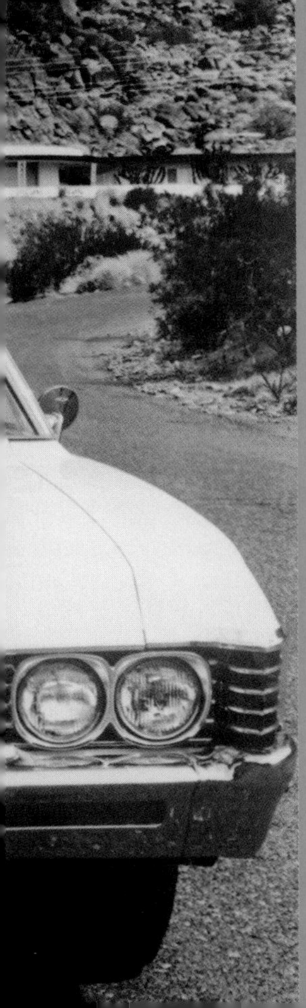

The man who has no

imagination has no wings.

Muhammad Ali

When a friend is in trouble, don't annoy him by asking if there is anything you can do. Think up something appropriate and do it.

Edgar Watson Howe

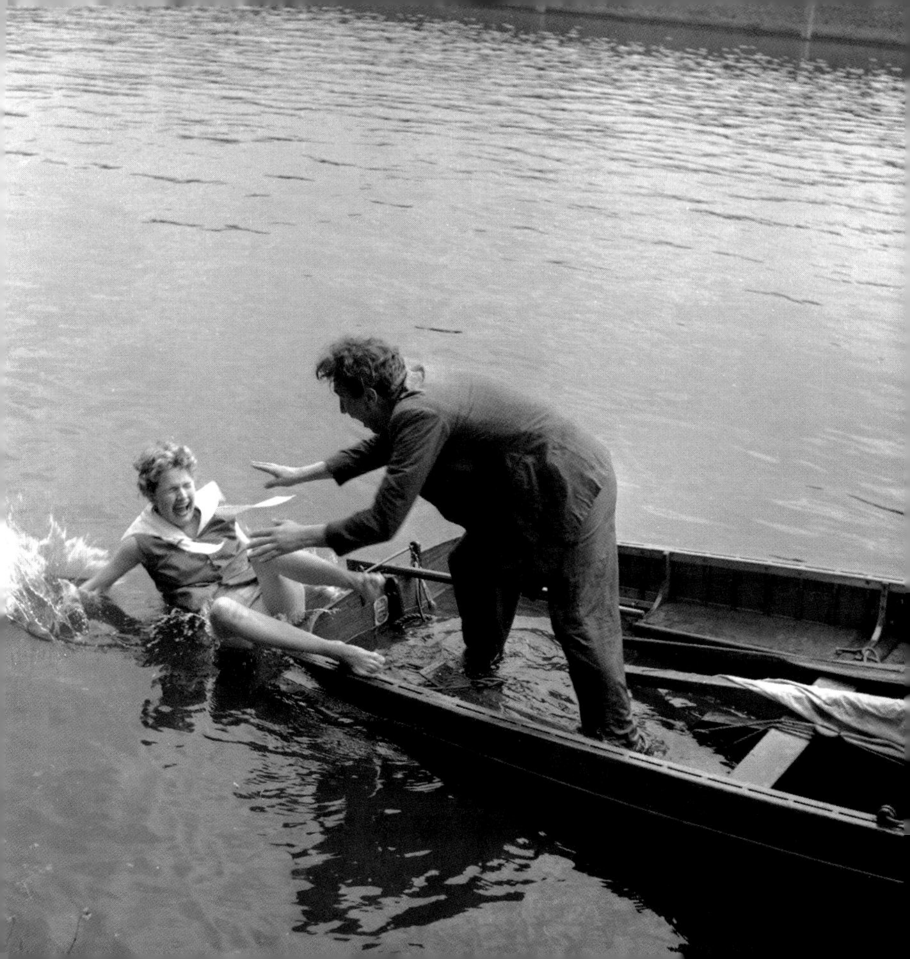

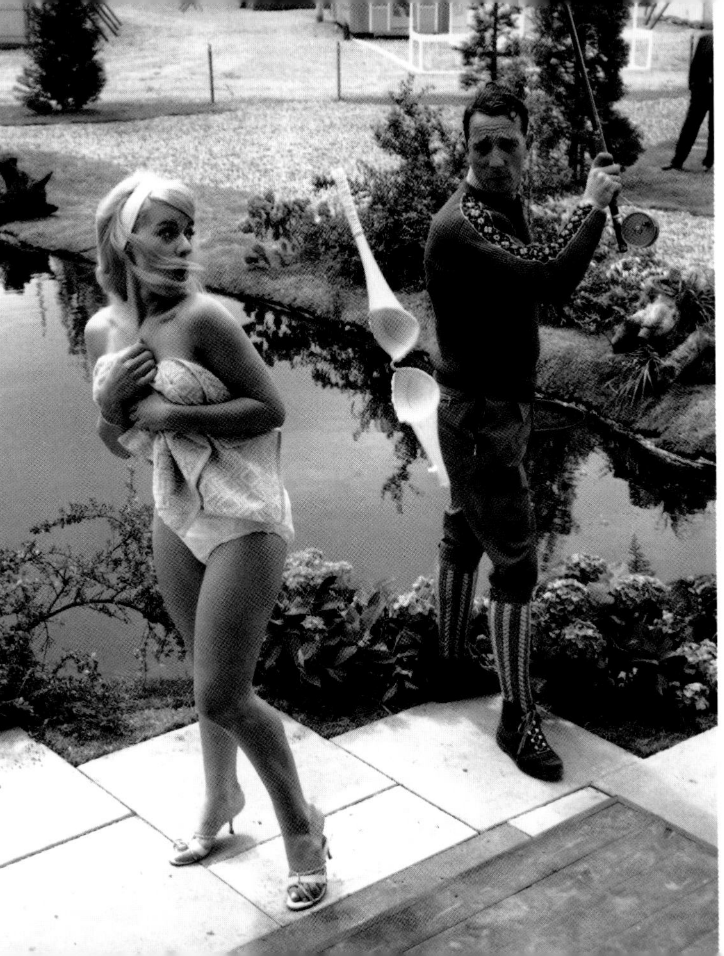

Suspense is worse than disappointment.

Robert Burns

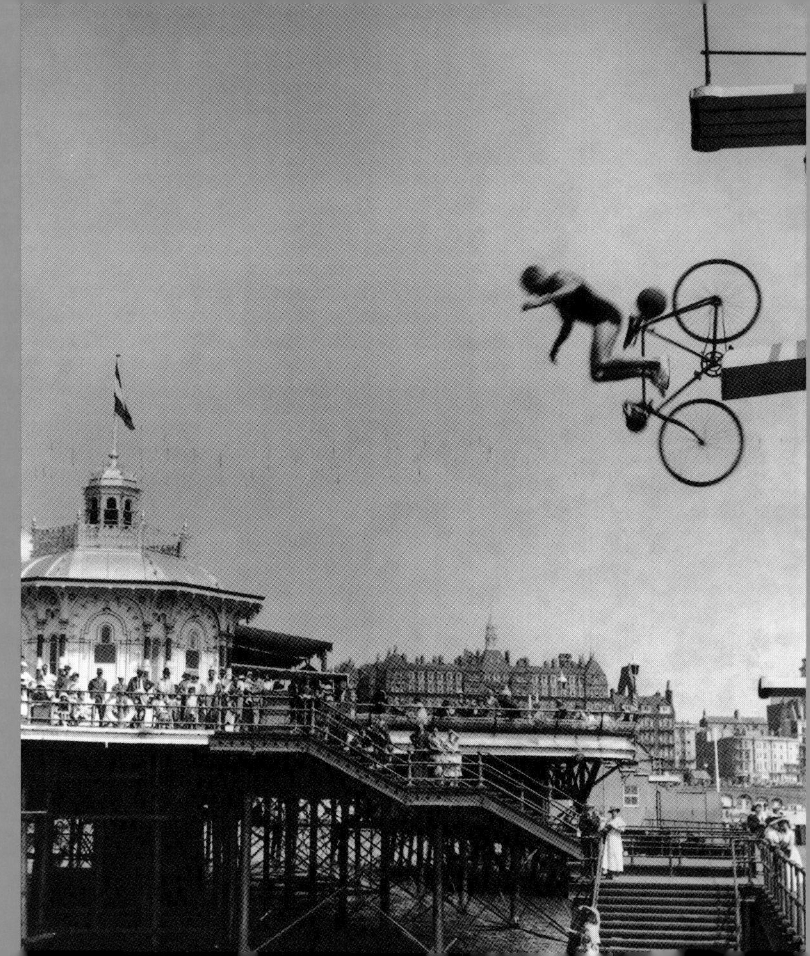

You must do the thing you think you cannot do.

Eleanor Roosevelt

Every exit is an entry somewhere else.

Tom Stoppard

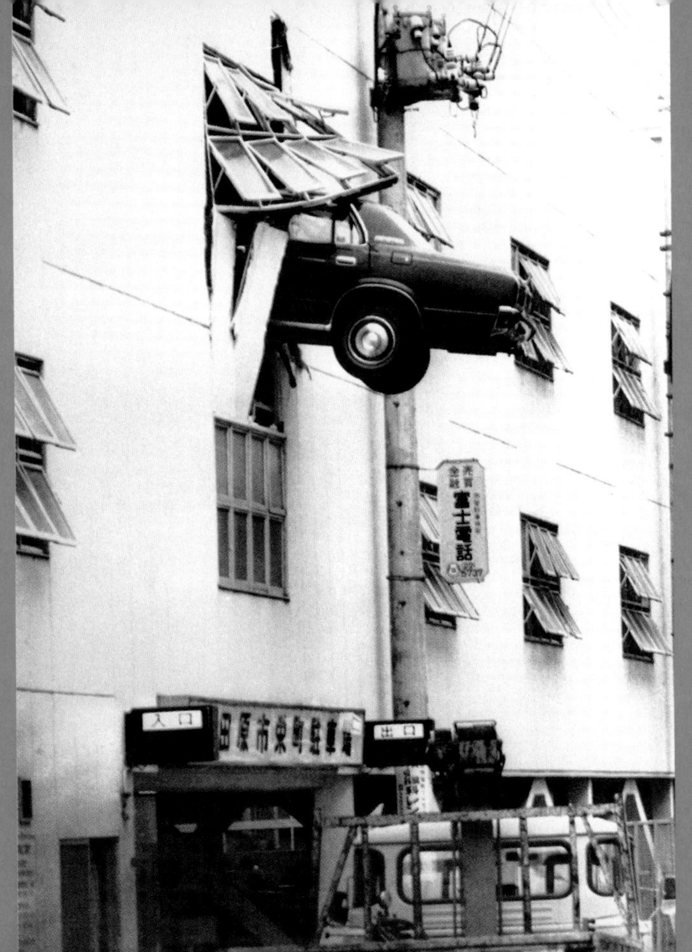
富士電話
入口
出口

Trust that still, small voice that says, "This might work and I'll try it."

Diana Mariechild

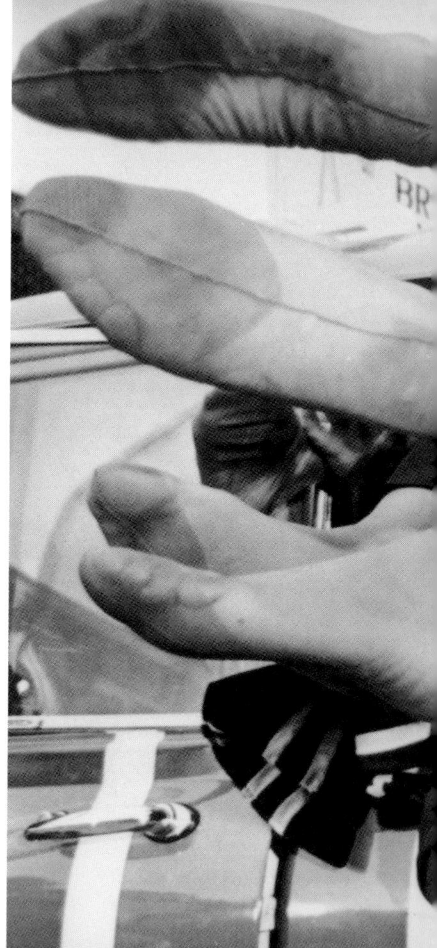

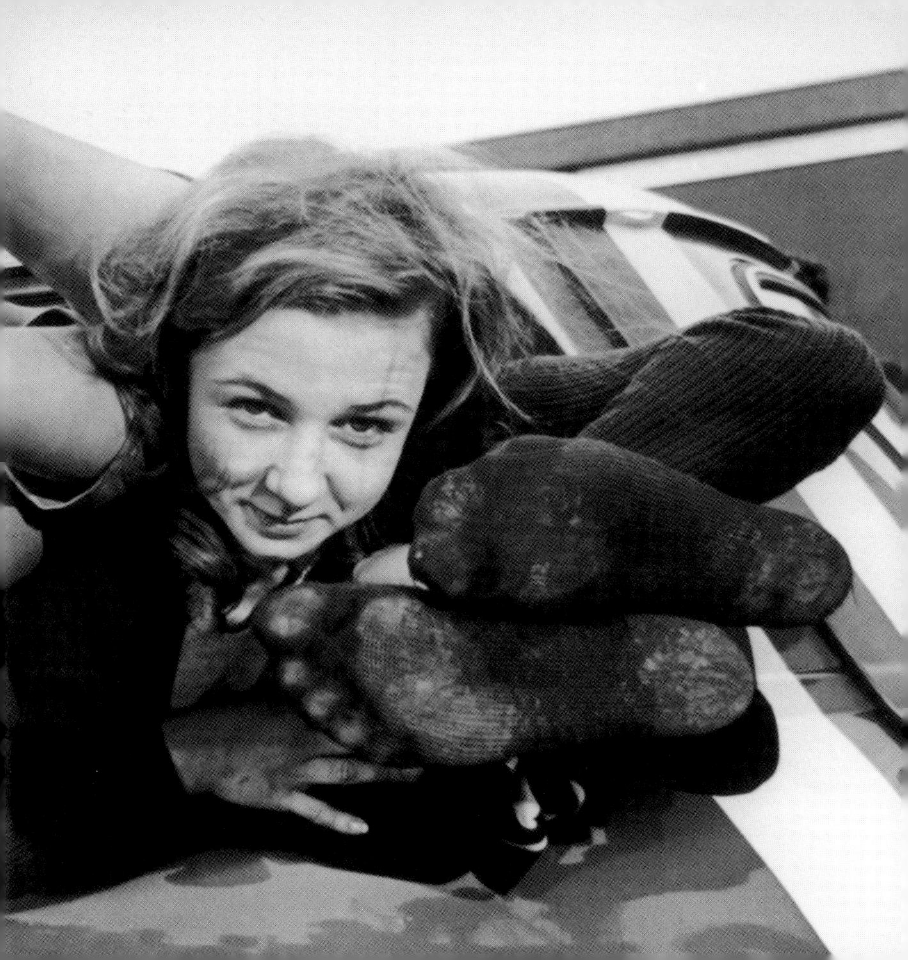

Picture Credits

All images Hulton Getty Picture Collection, unless otherwise specified.

cover:A young woman jumping into a lake, narrowly avoiding a rowing boat containing startled friends, circa 1950.

title page: Young female ice skater laughs while lying on the ice after a fall, circa 1945, © Lambert/Hulton Archive.

page 4: A man falls off his water-ski board, 1930.

page 7: British actress Evelyn Laye falls off a trolley during her birthday party at the London Country Club, Hendon, 1923.

page 8: An overturned bus on a road in Nigeria, ironically bearing the slogan, "Safe Journey," 1970.

page 10: A guardsman faints during the Trooping of the Colour ceremony held at Horse Guards Parade, London, to celebrate the official birthday of Queen Elizabeth II, 1957.

page 13: Three-year-old twins Bobby and Richard Pigg prove overly zealous in their garbage disposal in St. James' Park, London, 1952.

page 14: The veil of newly-wed bride Eileen Petticrew flies up in a gust of wind as she poses for photographs with husband Robert Greenhill, London, 1965.

page 16: British actor Michael Redgrave starts demolition of a building. His wife Rahael Kempson and actress Dame Peggy Ashcroft duck to avoid flying debris, 1971.

page 19: A member of the Addlestone women's cricket team missing a catch, 1924.

page 20: A house which has fallen onto the beach during a landslide caused by storms, UK, 1983, © The Observer.

page 23: Three young boys pull each other off a diving board, falling into a lake, circa 1955, © Lambert/Hulton Archive.

page 24: Dancer and model Jeann Marsh demonstrates some of the hazards which may beset those wearing stiletto heels, 1953.

page 26: Tamu, a baby elephant tries to get into a Mini, 1961.

page 28: A young musician relaxes in the shade of his instrument during a musical event at Miami University, Florida, 1966.

page 30: A submerged car which its drunken owner "parked" in a swimming pool in Beverly Hills, California, 1961.

page 33: A man falling backward on a broken front step of a house, circa 1945, © Lambert/Hulton Archive.

page 34: Mary Holmes receives a peck on the nose from a bird at the Formakin Animal Training School in Oxfordshire, UK, 1962.

page 37: A man holding a spanner remonstrates with a man popping his head out of a man-hole in the path of on-coming traffic, circa 1970.

page 39: A little girl takes delight in drenching her dad with shockingly cold water from the garden hose, 1936.

page 40: Orville Wright lands one of the early Wright gliders badly, overseen by his brother Wilbur, 1903.

page 42: A girl skater takes a tumble from the chair on which she was enjoying a ride on the frozen school lake, UK, 1933.

page 45: Babies playing on the lawn at Babies' Castle, a Dr Barnardo's charity home for orphans, 1938.

page 46: Actress and vocalist Doris Hare tries to climb out of a hammock at her cottage in Burgess Hill, Sussex, UK 1935.

page 49: Finnish rider R.A. Kuistila in the water after falling from his horse during the Equestrian Olympic Games in Stockholm, 1956.

page 51: Two women have an amusing accident whilst raking hay on a farm in Hatfield, UK, 1938.

page 52: Actor Harry Langdon and "The Horse Laugh," circa 1925.

page 54: A man asleep in a deckchair unaware of the incoming tide at Barry Island, near Cardiff, Wales, 1936.

page 56: A snowcat balanced precariously over a crevice, during a Trans-Atlantic Expedition, 1952.

page 59: Television producer Tony de Lotbiniere gets out of the way as an actor in Elizabethan costume draws his bow, 1953.

page 60: A woman is shocked and surprised by a revealing gust of wind in the funhouse at London's Battersea funfair, 1953.

page 63: John Lewis takes his pet swan Ziggy with him on his delivery rounds, 1962.

page 64: Roger Moore practices judo at Elstree Studios with teacher Barrie Shaigum, 1965.

page 66: Christine Child and Francis Pidgeon on the roof of Piccadilly Theatre after rehearsals for "The Crooked Mile," 1959.

page 68: A British racing car, driven by G. Ansell mid-air during a crash at Silverstone Grand Prix circuit, UK, 1948.

page 70: A pelican perches on an unsuspecting reader, 1964.

page 73: Chelsea pensioners on a helter-skelter, 1961.

page 75: Animal lover Olive Tate directing milk into her corgi dog Buster's mouth while milking a cow, 1963.

page 76: Two stacks of baskets come tumbling down during the porters' basket-carrying competition, London, 1951.

page 78: British boxer Jack Robinson falling over the ropes during his fight with Tommy Martin at the National Sporting Club's gala night at Earl's Court, London, 1938.

page 81: Two men making slow progress along the railings after the River Thames overflowed its banks in Putney, London, 1947.

page 82: Two women trying to rollerskate along the front at Hastings, UK, 1934.

page 85: Young skier Tamsin Herdman is amused after falling over on her skis in Edale, Derbyshire, UK, 1938.

page 87: Two dodgem car passengers are surprised to see Susie the circus bear bumping into them at the fun fair, London, 1954.

page 89: Children in fancy dress costume, though the one dressed as a nurse is taking it too seriously as she treats a "casualty," 1939.

page 90: Arnold Palmer battles to get out of a bunker at the Doral Eastern Open Golf Championships at Miami, 1970.

page 92: People cavorting in the snow at Lyndhurst Hill, Southampton, UK, 1978.

page 95: The Womans Auxiliary Police Corps in Preston, UK, working to keep a police car on the road, circa 1940.

page 97: Jockey Dan Byers falling off Acetis, the favourite in the Cedarhurst Steeplechase in Belmont Park, Long Island, 1926.

page 98: A car split in two halves on a road in Phoenix, Arizona. It was used by the AMT Corporation for a TV commercial, 1968.

page 101: British comedian Frankie Howard reaches out to a fellow passenger but fails to catch her before she falls in the water, 1954.

page 102: Actress Lesley Allen and actor Alex W. Caird put on a display for the press at Crystal Palace, London, 1965.

page 104: A stunt driver on a bicycle entertaining the crowds on Brighton sea front, UK, 1938.

page 107: A car protruding through the exterior wall after crashing in a third storey garage in Tokyo, 1977.

page 109: Brigitte Palmer leans out of the window of a Mini, surrounded by feet. She and 24 students from Chatham, UK, have crammed into a Mini in order to equal the world record, 1966.

Published by MQ Publications Limited
12 The Ivories, 6-8 Northampton Street, London N1 2HY
Tel: 020 7359 2244 / Fax: 020 7359 1616
email: mail@mqpublications.com

ISBN: 1-84072-315-7

3 5 7 9 0 8 6 4 2

Cover Design: John Casey
Design: Alexia Smith
Text research: David Baird
Picture research: Suzie Green
Series Editor: Kate John

Printed and bound in China